**On Determination:** "When I first came to the Hill, I immediately began lobbying members of Congress. I desperately wanted to be on the Judiciary Committee... there were also senior members vying for it and no openings. Then I heard that Barney Frank had just vacated his position...On January 28, 2003, I received a call that I'd landed the slot! So, once again I learned: never say never." **—Linda**

**On Commitment:** "I never complain anymore about having to fly, not getting enough sleep...If people want to speak to me, it's because they need something solved; they don't think that government listens to them, and they want answers. That's all part of the job." **—Loretta**

**On Giving 110 Percent:** "I frequently underestimate myself and what I'm capable of. However, throw me into a situation where I'm forced to produce out of my comfort zone and I can do it. You just have to believe you can rise to the occasion." **—Linda**

**On the Woman Who Inspired Them the Most:** "If Mom saw kids in the neighborhood who didn't have a jacket—kids who were much poorer than ourselves—she would go door-to-door, sell tamales, and raise the money to ensure these kids had galoshes and jackets. We were one of the poorest families in the area of Anaheim where we grew up, yet Mom always thought that others had far larger needs than we did." **—Loretta**

**...NOW LET THEM EMPOWER YOU!**

# DREAM
# *in* COLOR

## How the Sánchez Sisters Are
## Making History in Congress

**Congresswomen**

**Linda** *and* **Loretta Sánchez**

*with* **Richard Buskin**

**GRAND CENTRAL**
**PUBLISHING**

NEW YORK    BOSTON

Grand Central Publishing
Hachette Book Group USA
237 Park Avenue
New York, NY 10017

Visit our Web site at www.HachetteBookGroupUSA.com

Printed in the United States of America

First Edition: September 2008
10  9  8  7  6  5  4  3  2  1

Grand Central Publishing is a division of Hachette Book Group USA, Inc.
The Grand Central Publishing name and logo is a trademark of Hachette Book Group USA, Inc.

Library of Congress Cataloging-in-Publication Data

Sánchez, Loretta.
    Dream in color : how the Sánchez sisters are making history in Congress / Loretta and Linda Sánchez with Richard Buskin. – 1st ed.
        p. cm.
    ISBN: 978-0-446-50804-9
    1. Sánchez, Loretta.  2. Sánchez, Linda.  3. Women legislators–United States–Biography.  4. United States. Congress. House–Biography.  5. Mexican American women–Biography.  6. Sisters–United States–Biography.  I. Sánchez, Linda.  II. Buskin, Richard.  III. Title.
    E901.1.S26S26 2008
    328.092'2–dc22
    [B]
                                                        2007049593

Text design: Meryl Sussman Levavi

*To the strong women in our lives*
*who made us the women we are,*
*especially our grandmother, Amalia,*
*and our mother, Maria*

*To the girls who are developing their strength,*
*And the women who are still discovering theirs...*

# Contents

# Foreword

The story of Loretta and Linda Sánchez is one of perseverance and achievement. It renews my optimism in America's future.

The Congress I entered in 1987 was a different place from the one that serves the nation today. There were only eighteen women in both the House and Senate, compared to ninety today. There were fourteen members of Hispanic descent in the Congress, but not a single Hispanic woman. Congress looked little like the nation that it was elected to represent.

We have made great progress since then, thanks to the tenacity and determination of women and minorities who have fought to bring our nation closer to the ideal of equality which is both our heritage and our hope.

Loretta and Linda Sánchez are two of those tenacious fighters. Their story is one of many firsts. They are the first sisters – indeed the first women of any relation – to serve in Congress together. Loretta is the first woman and minority person to represent a district in Orange County, California; the first Head Start child to be elected to Congress; and the first woman to reach the highest positions on the Armed Services and Homeland Security committees in the House. Linda is the first Latina to serve on the House Judiciary Committee and the first woman ever to chair its Subcommittee on Commercial and Administrative Law.

Their story, however, is about more than electoral success and titles. Their story, and their family's story, is a quintessential *American* story. Their parents, who came to this country speaking almost no English, and without much money in their pockets, worked hard and eventually raised a family of seven. Their seven children went on to earn not only college degrees, but advanced degrees in business, finance, and law. This is essentially the same story as that of my Italian predecessors; it is the same story as that of the German, Irish, Polish, and other immigrants who came to our shores and enriched and strengthened our nation.

Ignorance, generalizations, and bigotry are sometimes allowed to obscure the tremendous contributions of immigrants. Instead, I choose to think of the story of a young Mexican immigrant, Alfredo Quinones-Hinojosa, who grew up picking fruit in California, eventually made his way to Harvard Medical School, and today works as a surgeon in my native Baltimore, dedicated to finding a cure for brain cancer. He is just one success story among so many.

Though Loretta and Linda each met resistance from those who said their dreams weren't rightfully theirs to dream, they defied the naysayers and blazed their own paths. Just as their parents enriched our nation, they are enriching the work of Congress—Loretta as a leader on issues of defense and homeland security, and Linda as a leader for social justice and civil rights.

Read on and enjoy getting to know Loretta and Linda, just as I have during my years working with them. They are two of the most dynamic women in Congress today. Their stories are candid, funny, and motivating. With this book, they have given us a great gift.

NANCY PELOSI
*Speaker of the U.S. House of Representatives*

# DREAM
## *in* COLOR

# 1

## Mi Casa Es Su Casa

In 1851, Israel Washburn was elected to Congress. Two years later, Elihu Washburne joined him in the House of Representatives. Perhaps the extra *e* at the end of Elihu's last name prevented people from realizing it at the time, but these were the first brothers ever to serve in Congress.

About a century later, a young Mexican woman made the decision to head north in pursuit of a better life. If she had been informed during that exhausting journey, when her future was just a giant question mark, that two of her seven yet-to-be-born children would become the first sisters in the American Congress, she would have been incredulous. And yet, that's exactly what happened.

In January 2003, precisely 150 years after the aforementioned brothers' names were written into the history books, Loretta and Linda Sánchez, daughters of immigrants Maria Macias and Ignacio Sánchez, became the first sisters in Congress. Before this, 1,881 relatives had served in the House, but never sisters. Why did it take so long? And what enabled us to finally break through this most resilient of barriers?

Of course, we're delighted to be the first and, so far, only sisters on Capitol Hill, but we're also disheartened. As we stride down the halls of the Longworth Building, racing to the next vote, why don't we see more faces like our own, female or Latino? Anyone who's glanced at recent U.S. population statistics knows that the word *minority* is rapidly becoming a misnomer, as 35 million Hispanics certainly don't sound all that minor to us. Okay, so we're the exception. But we shouldn't be. And that's why we want to tell our story—to inspire others to pursue a career in public service, and to ultimately speed up the sluggish transition to a more representative government.

Step into our world, both political and personal, and take a behind-the-scenes look at our joint and individual experiences. After all, despite sharing the same background and many similar views, we're also two very distinct individuals: Loretta the businesswoman,

Linda the lawyer; Loretta the neat freak, Linda the leave-it-where-it-drops specialist; Loretta the exercise-conscious early riser, Linda the late stop-out who's returning home just as her big sister is getting up. It would make for some engaging interaction if we shared a home together in Washington, D.C.

## LORETTA

To a certain extent we grew up together, but in many ways we didn't. I'm the second among seven kids, Linda's number six, and the older siblings usually stayed together and the younger ones played together. However, the older ones also had to take care of the younger ones, so from changing Linda's diapers when she was a baby to watching over her and our youngest brother, Michael, when our mom had to work or run errands, I served as a sort of surrogate mother.

## LINDA

She always had her soapbox and was preaching about eating the right food, doing chores, and taking care of ourselves to the point where sometimes I felt like I might as well be living in a convent. She was not only a caregiver, but a disciplinarian as well. While our parents were stricter with the older siblings and more lenient by the time they got around to us, it was the older siblings who were super strict with the younger. Still, I don't think I ever consciously thought about defying them. In Latino families, there's a lot of deference given by younger kids to older siblings, because you're supposed to respect authority. So, while Loretta might recall me disobeying her, I didn't ever purposely resist what she told me to do.

## LORETTA

I'd agree with that. When there are seven kids, you have to keep control or chaos will ensue, and so there was a lot of discipline in our home. Having been raised strictly myself, I was the same with the younger set when I was in charge. I was responsible for them, and I tried to use the same parenting techniques that I saw my mom use. I think Linda used to call me the Witch.

## LINDA

Actually, it was the Warden. While Henry was the firstborn among the siblings, for all intents and purposes Loretta was the eldest. She was the one who took charge.

## LORETTA

That's largely because Henry is an artist and a dreamer. As the head guy he always took the brunt of our parents' discipline. He was expected to do everything right, and for the most part he did. But at the same time, being a dreamer, he didn't want to be in control of the younger kids, so he handed that responsibility to me.

## LINDA

On Saturdays we had to get up and do chores. I think our parents' philosophy was that if we were busy we'd be too tired to get into trouble. So, they pushed us to study, to be involved in sports, and, on Saturday mornings, to do chores around the house. Mom would go into the kitchen at some ungodly hour and quite literally rattle the pots and pans as an alarm clock, and then Loretta would act as the overseer, checking to make sure we weren't goofing off, then reporting back on our performance! That's why she was the Warden.

## LORETTA

I was the one with white gloves. I did my own chores, but I also had to make sure everyone else stayed in line.

## LINDA

We didn't actually rebel, but revenge was sometimes exacted on her. We knew, for example, that Loretta was deathly afraid of June bugs, so we'd place them on her face while she was asleep or tangle them in her hair, and then watch as she screamed and Dad held her down, trying to pull each of them out.

## LORETTA

Initially, my role was to help prevent chaos, account for everybody, and keep the home orderly, because my mother had so many things to do. But eventually, as I began experiencing things that our parents had never experienced, I turned into a sort of advance scout for the younger siblings.

For example, right from the start our parents wanted all of their kids to go to college, but when I had to decide which college to attend, Dad said it should be USC, where Henry was already going. The reason? "They have a good football team!" He had no idea about choosing a college based on our interests and what classes were being offered. He could only relate to it in the way that he knew. I didn't know much either, because my school counselors hardly acknowledged that I'd even make it to college.

There was no one to advise me which place would be best suited to what I wanted to do and how I wanted to do it, whereas by the time Linda got to that same point and was thinking of applying to Cal State Fullerton, I said, "What are you talking about? You can go to Cal Berkeley, you can go to Brown University, you can go to

Harvard." She said, "But I'm not smart enough to get into those colleges," to which I rolled my eyes and responded, "You're smart enough to get into *all* of those colleges! It's just a matter of what you want to study." I asked her what she liked about school, and after that, I gave her a list of about ten different schools to which she should apply.

## LINDA

Although Dad wanted his girls to go to college, he also wanted us to go to Cal State Fullerton down the street—which he described as "one of the best universities in the country"—so that we'd still be living at home, where he could keep an eye on us. It didn't matter where the boys went. That's why, when I eventually decided to go to a college in San Francisco, we didn't even tell my father. Mom and I supposedly went "on vacation" to visit some relatives up north, but what we really did was drive up to Berkeley to find me an apartment. Then, two days before classes were due to begin, as I packed everything into my little car, Dad asked, "Where are you going?" I said, "I'm going to college." When he learned it was Berkeley he was not happy, but it was too late. I'd already enrolled and paid my tuition, so there was no way I could back out. Mom, Loretta, and I had conspired to do this, and we all got an earful, but what could he do? I was going to one of the best schools in California, and since my father's extremely thrifty with a dollar he'd never waste the money by saying I couldn't go there.

## LORETTA

I wanted Linda, and the rest of my brothers and sisters, to not have to reinvent the wheel. I'd walked around blindly, trying to figure out many of those things, and I didn't want them to have the same experience. In my case, when Dad initially told me to go to USC like my older brother Henry, I took a look and didn't believe it fit me well. When I got home I told Dad and he said, "That's okay, Loretta. There's this great little community college that I pass every single day on the way home. Its name is Chapman, and it looks so nice, I think you should check it out." So, I did go and check it out, and I immediately discovered it wasn't a community college, it was a private four-year university. That meant instead of costing $5 per unit, as Dad thought it would, the annual fee was $8,000. That was a lot of money in 1978, and didn't exactly fit the plan to work and pay for it all by myself.

When I arrived home, I told Dad, "I really, really like that school. I think it's a good fit for me and I want to go there...Oh, and by the way, it's not a community college, and it costs eight thousand dollars a year." He about choked. Still, I did end up going there. I received a federal Pell grant, a state grant, and a private scholarship from a family, the Pralles, that helped kids attend college, and so it cost my parents nothing. Some people go to Harvard or Stanford or Cal Berkeley because their parents have already gone there, other relatives have already gone there, and family money has resulted in their names being given to some of the halls. We didn't have that kind of background, so we had to make it on our own, usually with the help of families we didn't know but who understood how important education was for everyone.

It was much the same with politics. I went through the experience of running for Congress first, although politics is much more in Linda's blood than it is in mine. However, it obviously helped that, by the time she decided to run for Congress, I was already there and I already knew the ropes. In fact, when she said, "I want to do this," one of the deciding factors was that I had developed an infrastructure—what I call the good ol' girl network—that she could use to set up her campaign and win.

## LINDA

I remember the day I called Loretta and said, "Are you sitting down?" "What's up?" she asked, to which I replied, "The new congressional seat that's just been created in my area—I want to run for it." There was this pregnant pause at the other end of the line. Then she said, "Well, I don't know, Linda. What's your strategy for winning? How are you going to raise the money? There's that assemblywoman who represents a large portion of the district." As she herself has since decribed it, it was like having your best friend hire your child—you want your kid to understand there'll be no easy treatment just because of the friendship.

Loretta was basically saying, "Do you realize what this involves?" and my response was "Look, you travel all over the United States, and you campaign for candidates who, in some cases, you've barely met. You're always talking about how we need more qualified women in office, and how we need more Latinos in office to reflect this country's diversity, and you know my background. You know I'm qualified, with all my legal training and experience working for the labor movement."

She said, "Okay, well, let me think about it." Then, the next day, she called and said, "You know what, Linda, you're right. I'm going to help you." Which she did, of course. She continued to help even after I'd entered the House, assisting in my effort to secure a slot on the Judiciary Committee, making recommendations when I was setting up my office, and generally showing me the lay of the land. Then again, there were also times when my big sister still brought along her soapbox...

One time, I was sitting on the floor of the House, and between votes I was talking trade with a couple of male colleagues when Loretta came up, stood right in front of me, and said, "Linda, have you had your flu shot yet?" I was in mid-sentence, talking to these guys, so I signaled no, only for her to then wag her finger at me and say, "Today's the last day that the House physician is giving the flu shot, and you have a tendency to get sick when you're flying back and forth. You'd better get your shot right away!" There I was, discussing a serious issue with my colleagues, and I felt like a kid being told to put on clean underwear. But that's Loretta—part mother, part sister.

## LORETTA

Hey, what's wrong with that? When we were growing up, our dad used whatever was going on to teach us very, very valuable lessons, and as a result the siblings would never discount things that could be learned from each other. We have always learned from each other and helped each other. So, as much as I look out for Linda, I also often go to her for advice. She, after all, is the real lawyer. I just watch *Law & Order*. And although I generally understand how things work from a legal standpoint, I still consult her when it gets down to the nitty-gritty of interpreting the law. That's her background, that's her training…and I also go to her when she has better contacts to a House member that I need to reach out to. We're not competitive with one another or with any of our siblings. On the contrary, I'm her biggest cheerleader, and she's mine.

That having been said, for Linda and me to share a home together in Washington, D.C., it would have to be one of those places that, in addition to a common area, has an east wing and a west wing, enabling us to reside as far apart as possible!

## LINDA

Because of all the years I was in law school, my favorite, most productive time is usually from about nine in the evening until one or two in the morning.

## LORETTA

And that's my favorite, most productive time to sleep.

## LINDA

Loretta is one of those crazy, fanatical early morning people who gets up at five, which I think is unnatural. So, heaven help her if I were to get to bed at two in the morning and then hear her rattling around the house at five.

## LORETTA

I've often thought we could share a single bedroom. I would use the bed while she's up, and as I'd be rolling out she'd be coming in.

## LINDA

Since Loretta's not a real late-night person, if I'm grabbing dinner with a colleague at 8:30 in the evening, that's about the same time she's ready to walk home, do some reading, and go to bed.

## LORETTA

Dinner always sounds like a good idea at 8:15 when we're about to vote. But then, after the vote, when it's 8:45 and we're standing around, I'm like, "Man, I need to go home and sleep now."

Right after the vote my on switch turns to off. And that means while I'm chilling out at home, Linda's socializing, making friends, and talking to our colleagues.

I have a different set of friends, because they're the ones who get up at five in the morning to go for a run, before getting to the gym at 6:00 a.m. And you can also get a lot of business done at the gym in the morning with your colleagues, because again it's a different set of people. So, if Linda doesn't know somebody, I probably do, and vice versa. Between us, we know them all, and that's really good in Washington, where work takes place all the time. People there don't have another topic of conversation!

## LINDA

Well, that's not entirely true. I'm on the Democrats' baseball team, and when I'm with those guys we might talk ball for ten minutes.

## LORETTA

Yes, and in my case we might talk about the musical I saw last night. There are a lot of renaissance people in the Congress, and I pretty much consider myself to be a source for what's going on. However, usually when we're together it's a time for us to bounce ideas off each other, talk politics at home — "How should I handle this?" "What do you think of that?" "How do we get to the eighteen-to-twenty-four-year-olds who are in rehab right now?" So much of it is shop talk.

## LINDA

It definitely gets to a point where I've had enough talking about politics. In fact, when I go back to California and I catch up with my cousins or my friends, over dinner they'll ask me what I'm working on and at first I won't mind telling them. However, after about thirty minutes I'll suddenly stop that conversation by saying, "So, are you dating anybody?" I don't want to stay on the subject of politics all the time, and if the conversation returns there I'll then ask someone, "How are your parents?"

## LORETTA

Of course, there are many times when we discover that someone at a social get-together is actually there because of his or her political agenda. I try to tell them, "I'm not going to remember whatever it is you're saying. *Call my staff.* They know much more about this subject than I do." They somehow think that, at the office the next morning, you're going to remember the hundred different things that people asked you to do the night before, even if it's arranging a tour for visiting D.C.

## LINDA

What bothers me a lot is that some people who know me want to talk about my job all the time but never ask, "How are *you* doing, Linda?" or "How's your family?" Those who've known me a long time generally will, but not all the new friends I've acquired since being elected. Some are only interested in my professional life; they never consider I might have other interests in addition to politics.

## LORETTA

Some people are just curious, I think, and that's understandable. We're very accessible, and so it's natural for them to ask questions. I usually just handle it in a different way from Linda. I'll start off by regaling them with a couple of really funny stories relating to the Congress so they can have a good laugh and feel like they've got that tidbit of inside information. Then, after that, they can get on with just being themselves and not have to ask anything else. I think they just want the "inside scoop" on Congress. Actually, every day is exciting in Congress. So, why not?

## LINDA

As you can tell, Loretta and I have quite distinct personalities. But then, we also share several traits: optimism, an affinity for risk taking, a sense of adventure, and a work ethic that I think we and our siblings inherited from our parents, the immigrant work ethic.

## LORETTA

Recently I was standing in the lobby of a building in the city of Orange, where I was scheduled to speak in front of the Orange County women judges, and there were other people attending a meeting of the city's Heritage Foundation in the next room, which by definition is fairly Anglo, conservative, and wealthy. Anyway, some senior guy came over to me and asked, "Are you Loretta Sánchez?" I said, "Yes, sir, I am," and he said, "I've been meaning to talk to you for a while." I was thinking, "Great. Okay, let me have it," assuming he wanted to discuss immigration or something like that, but instead he said, "I used to own a company in the rubber-plastics industry and I know your father, Ignacio, and I just want to tell you he was the hardest-working man I've ever known in my entire life."

It was humbling. He went on and on about how my dad gave 100 percent every day, how you could call him at five in the morning and he'd be there right away, and how he always got the job done. He asked, "Is your dad still alive?" and I said, "Yes, he's got Alzheimer's." It really gets to me emotionally when people I've never met before describe the impact my father has made on their lives. And I'm also moved by how respectful they are of him, even though he was a blue-collar worker.

## LINDA

With this book I hope we, too, can make an impact, inspiring people and helping them understand what it takes to get things done.

## LORETTA

It's also about the self-belief that our mom and dad instilled in us. They thought we could be whatever we wanted to be—Madame Curie on a spaceship! That applies to everyone. You've got to allow yourself to dream, and then you must exploit the ways in which to achieve that. The people who realize their goals are the people who outlast all the naysayers and any negativity that surrounds them. And you also have to be yourself. Washington is very stifling in terms of the way others want you to act...

## LINDA

...and want you to look and want you to speak. One thing that people are invariably attracted to is confidence. There's a theory that you're not born lucky or unlucky, but that you make your own luck. Well, when you have confidence in terms of knowing who you are, what you're about, and what you want to accomplish, people are drawn to that, so long as you're not cocky or arrogant. One thing I've learned in Washington is that you don't have to conform to other people's ideas of what you should be. That will only erode your confidence, whereas by being yourself and being unorthodox you'll stand out for all the right reasons. Not only will you attract attention for being a little out of the ordinary, but your confidence will be infectious.

In a million subtle and not-so-subtle ways you're constantly being told what you *should* be like. Fashion magazines tell you what you should look like and self-help books tell you how you should think, and everything's built around this expectation that you will be—or aspire to be—something that other people envision for you. Lord knows, this is true for me. I'm not a size 4, nor, probably, will I ever be, but I have a lot to offer in terms of intellect and passion and compassion. And even if I'm unfamiliar with a particular situation or environment, I know who I am, what my values are, and what I want to do, and I'll persevere until I get it done. I hope that's one of the messages our story conveys— you don't have to be a supermodel to stand out from the crowd. Everyone can make an incredible difference in this world, and it doesn't matter if you're part of a minority, from humble beginnings, or started out with more obstacles than the average person. Loretta and I have had to overcome all those challenges, and we've learned as young women who got elected to Congress just how important it is to be the person that you fundamentally are.

# 2

## Let Your Roots Show

Many people work hard to conceal their background, conforming or projecting themselves in ways that are deemed socially acceptable, politically correct, physically desirable, or otherwise in vogue. And women and minorities are often more prone to this, partly because they're taught to aspire to some mythical ideal. Not us.

Growing up in a traditional Mexican family, we learned about the rich cultural values of our heritage, and as Latinas in Congress we draw daily strength from the lessons that our parents instilled in us. One of the strongest examples of such a lesson is the way Mom stood her ground when told by one of our grade school teachers that we should speak only English at home. She knew that being bilingual was an asset, and we have both repeatedly reaped the benefits of her foresight. After all, aside from Loretta, how many members of the House's Armed Forces Committee can communicate directly with foreign counterparts during official missions? And, aside from Linda, how many House members have been invited to give the Spanish Democratic response to the State of the Union address only two weeks after entering Congress?

Being in the public eye isn't easy. You're judged and evaluated constantly. We've been criticized for being so open about who we are, for speaking our minds, for sisterly bickering in front of reporters, even for wearing our stiletto heels to work. However, there's no way we're going to change to meet others' expectations. We are who we are—no apologies, no excuses. And if our close family bonds, our faith, and the strong work ethic we inherited from our parents all stem from our Latino roots, we're more than proud to let them show.

## LINDA

From an early age, I appreciated the beauty of knowing a second language and a second culture. Our parents constantly emphasized the importance of embracing who we are, and thanks to that I developed the confidence to resist trying to be like everyone else.

One of my best memories of Mom demonstrating her strength, her pride, and her values stems from her attending "Back to School Night" and meeting my teacher when I was in first grade. During the mid-seventies, Mexican students were still discouraged from speaking Spanish at school—the emphasis was on looking, acting, and sounding just like all the other kids. So, when I showed Mom a picture that I'd painted and the two of us conversed in Spanish, my teacher was horrified: "Oh no, no, no, Mrs. Sánchez! You must speak to your children in English or they will never learn the language!"

"My children come to school to learn English," Mom replied. "It's your job to teach them English. At home, we speak Spanish, and that way when they grow up they will know both languages."

That night I learned a valuable lesson: stand up for your convictions, even if they aren't popular. And to this day, I admire Mom for bucking the system and insisting that we learn both our adopted and native languages. The French have an expression that translates as "A person who knows two languages has the value of two," and that's certainly been my experience. My ability to speak two languages and understand two cultures has been invaluable. It has helped me in every job I've ever held, and I can't recall a single employer who wasn't glad to have access to this kind of expertise. On the other hand, I've known kids who were told to learn only English, and consequently they relinquished not only the opportunity to be bilingual, but also an important connection to their heritage and their ancestry.

When people ask me what I liked best about my childhood, I tell them, "Growing up in a large family." I don't even have to stop and think about that. There were, of course, times when I wished I had my own room. With so many brothers and sisters, real privacy was out of the question, and I often resented having to wear hand-me-downs or play with old toys. However, the closeness that our family shared—and still shares—was well worth the drawbacks.

As hard as they worked, our parents always ensured we spent quality time together, even if this meant sitting down to eat in shifts at our tiny, four-person kitchen table. On weeknights, we'd discuss what each of us had learned or done in school that day. And on weekends we'd always have activities that revolved around the family unit. After completing our Saturday morning chores, we'd have lunch together and then the afternoon would be ours. I loved the freedom of those afternoons, playing with other kids on our street, riding our bikes to explore the orange groves and vacant lots where we created inclines for bike jumps, and playing hide-and-seek.

Our Sunday ritual commenced with getting ready for church. Since there were so many of us and we only had one bathtub, Mom would save time by bathing us the night before. She'd set the girls' hair in rag rollers—my sisters helped me with mine—and then select and lay our clothes out for the next morning. There was a precision and efficiency to everything she did, and the result was that all seven kids were invariably ready for eight o'clock Mass at St. Anthony's. All nine of us would head there in our brown Dodge van, and it never ceased to amaze the priests or the regular congregants that the Sánchez family always made it to church on time, with everyone well groomed and the kids on their best behavior.

Our parents are both devout Catholics. From the time I was little, in addition to attending Sunday Mass, I also remember studying Catechism on Tuesday evenings. Mom and Dad thought it was important for us to grow up with a set of religious and moral values by which to live. But, they were also very tolerant of other religious views, and always believed that the way you live your life is far more important than religious dogma. Mom viewed her faith as a means of keeping life's joys and hardships in perspective. She learned from her mother, Amalia, that faith is to be savored during both good times and bad. My grandmother and mother— each of whose lives had encompassed numerous difficulties— developed a belief that, without faith, there's no hope for the future.

Amalia was the family matriarch, and, as such, she took our religious upbringing to heart. When I was old enough to drive, she asked me if I wouldn't mind taking her to church, because by that time she was using a cane and had trouble walking. At first I resisted—it would mean getting up extra early on Sunday (*never* my forte) and driving an hour to her house, and an hour back. But then, realizing that my grandmother wouldn't be around forever, I agreed.

Those Sundays with her helped shape many of the values I have today. As we sat listening to Spanish-language Mass, she'd make mental notes for later discussion. Then, after church, we'd go to lunch — usually at a Chinese restaurant or a diner where all the waitresses had beehive hairdos — and chat about what we'd just learned. The thing is, Grandma's take on the "lesson of the day" was often a little different from what the priest had actually said, and that's because she'd embellish the words of his sermon with the wisdom culled from her own experiences.

Take the time when the priest urged women to "obey their husbands." Afterward, Grandma told me, "*Mija* [my girl], the Bible may say that you should obey your husband, but God made you with a mind and spirit all your own. Do not squander the talents he has given you, and do not feel you ever have to submit to someone whose opinions may not be right. Think for yourself, search your soul, and trust in God when you are in doubt." She had seen too many young women marry, start families, and find themselves trapped in unhappy — even abusive — situations, unable to get out of them because of the stigma attached to a Latina who doesn't obey her husband.

My many Sundays with Grandma taught me that religion is about more than being able to quote the Scriptures; it's about trusting your own conscience and believing that God created each of us with a mind and freedom to make decisions. When things go particularly well on any given day, I always thank God silently for my good fortune. When things go poorly on any given day, I trust that they'll improve, that I just have to work harder and keep the faith. I'm not given to public displays of faith, and I don't believe you have to pray publicly to be righteous—I just carry within me my mother's and grandmother's belief that without faith there's no hope for the future.

When I was little, Sunday morning Mass would often be followed by family afternoons in the park, where our parents would invite our cousins and neighbors to barbecue with us. To their way of thinking, it was extremely important for us to appreciate our family and also know our extended clan. They believed that each of us possessed special talents and skills, and that if we worked together there was no obstacle that we—and our extended family—couldn't overcome. Experience had taught them that people often look down on those who come from different cultures, so they always reinforced the importance of sticking together, especially since there were so few Mexican families where we lived.

Our parents had a tough life, and we grew up with few luxuries, yet they always took time to enjoy what they were blessed with: seven healthy kids, loads of good friends, and life in the land of opportunity. There was plenty of laughter in our modest three-bedroom home and everyone was welcome, with the kitchen table serving as a gathering place for friends, neighbors, playmates, and friends of friends. That having been said, I'm also convinced that Mom's culinary skills played a large part in our popularity. People would visit because they knew they'd get fed, have plenty of company, and feel the warm hospitality that's reflected in the Latino adage *mi casa es su casa*.

Mom and Dad especially loved it when friends or neighbors brought out of towners over to our house. Since we didn't have the money to travel to places like New York, Kansas, or Mississippi, they believed that entertaining people from other places was a way of bringing those places to us. And let's face it, if there's anything out of towners like better than a home-cooked meal, it's the chance to talk about their own home and the people who'll be waiting for them when they return. Our parents understood that you could learn a lot from people of different cultures and backgrounds, and they also knew that people with different perspectives and experiences make life more interesting. That's why our front door was almost never locked, with people wandering in and out at will.

Everyone felt so at home in our kitchen that Mom once returned early from work to find a sixteen-year-old neighbor sitting at our kitchen table, eating leftovers out of our refrigerator that he had warmed on the stove even though no one else was around. She still laughs about that. You see, I think she secretly enjoys knowing that her cooking made her famous in our neighborhood, and that our friends considered her their "second mom." It's a testament to her hospitality and to the fun people had whenever they were in our home. Everyone who visited us was treated like family.

My mother is one of the most generous people I know. She has a good heart and is always willing to lend a hand when others are in need. From time to time, one of my brothers' or sisters' friends would be in trouble—perhaps they weren't getting along with their parents—and Mom would take them in for a few days until things cooled down. She always let their parents know where they were, and at the same time she'd counsel her "adoptees" about how much those parents did for them, making sure to point out that "there's nothing more hurtful to a parent than an ungrateful child."

Mom's generosity also extended to complete strangers. I can't recall a time when she didn't open her purse to give something—no matter how little she had—to the homeless or people down on their luck. She knew what it was like to grow up poor, and that a few dollars could make the difference in terms of having something to eat. I remember stopping at a gas station during my early teens and someone asking Mom for spare change. Without hesitation, she opened her wallet and handed the man a ten-dollar bill—a significant amount of money for us at that time. I couldn't believe it.

"Why did you do *that?*" I asked. "He's only going to spend it on alcohol or drugs!"

Mom looked at me for a long moment. Then she said, "Linda, I have no way of knowing what he'll use the money for. The point is, he needs it. That's enough for me. If I spent my life trying to judge who was worthy of help, I'd probably overlook someone truly in need. I don't want to live with the thought that I could have made a difference but chose not to."

I have never forgotten those words, and today I still try to live up to my mother's example.

When our parents talked about giving something back to others, I knew they didn't just mean charitable giving. They meant giving of yourself. From the very start, they let us know that, although we weren't blessed with much, it was certainly more than others had, and that with a good education we'd enjoy ample opportunity to better ourselves. They expected great things from us. Still, despite the prospect of our having far more financial security than they had, they also stressed that money was not the measure of success. "Once you've made it in this country," one of them would say, "you have an obligation to turn around and help those behind you."

Mom always helped others in whatever way she could, and she was outraged when, during the immigration amnesty of the 1980s, she learned that so-called notaries were charging people between $200 to $1,000 to fill out basic citizenship application forms. As a bilingual aide who had plenty of immigrant students in her class, she knew all about the struggle that their parents endured to make ends meet. And the fact that they were now paying exorbitant fees to charlatans not even qualified in immigration law was more than she could take.

Every Saturday, she would set up a typewriter at the dining room table and help people fill out the paperwork. And since I was taking a typing course in high school, I was the designated typist. Throughout the day, a steady stream of students' parents and friends of friends would come to our house for help. Mom would offer them coffee and sweet bread, take time to explain what was required, and answer whatever questions they might have. She treated gardeners the same as doctors, field workers the same as skilled tradesmen—with equal respect and affection for all. And she never charged anyone a cent for her assistance. Their relief and gratitude were payment enough. Working alongside Mom, I came to understand how little things could make a big difference in people's lives. In fact, my experience assisting with these immigration applications was one of the things that influenced my decision to become an attorney and help my community.

My parents had a strict rule in our house regarding work. Work was to be shared, and there was plenty of it to go around. When we each turned fifteen, Dad insisted that we get a part-time job for a few hours a week to learn the value of money. Sure, school was still our number one focus, but he wanted us to learn what it means to work in order to buy the things that you want.

Whereas my brothers went to work with Dad at his machine shop, my older sisters got jobs in retail—Loretta scooped ice cream at the local Sav-On drugstore and Martha sold doughnuts at Winchell's. I, on the other hand, was fascinated with welding and tools and what my father did for a living. So, when I turned fifteen, I asked if I could go to work with him at the machine shop. Initially, I think he was a little taken aback by this, but he agreed, instructing me to dress in my oldest clothes and be up at six o'clock on Saturday morning. And that's what happened. The following Saturday, my younger brother Mike and I, wearing sweatpants and faded T-shirts, went to work with our father.

Dad gave Mike the task of sorting tools and materials in the shop, but he seemed a little perplexed as to what job he should assign me. Probably confounded by the fact that I was a girl, he decided to have me do "women's work"—sweeping up metal shavings from the floor, degreasing some pieces of machinery, and stripping paint off oxyacetylene tanks. In other words, he went out of his way to give me the dirtiest, most tedious cleaning jobs he could think of, and by the end of the day I was hot, exhausted, and filthy. In fact, my hands were so wrecked that, no matter how much Lava soap I used to remove the grease, some of it remained under my fingernails—definitely not attractive for a girl.

"Look at these," Dad said, showing me his own hands, which had scars, calluses, and permanent half-moons of grease under the nails. "If you don't go to college, this is what yours will look like for the rest of your life. However, if you do go to college, someday you'll work in a big office with a nice view. You will go to work in a suit, *toda perfumada* [smelling of perfume], and you will have your own secretary to bring you coffee."

Years later, after I'd graduated from law school and was working for a firm in Orange County that afforded me my own office and a view of the beach, I heard an ad for Secretary's Day on the car radio and made a mental note to get something for my own assistant. Then, as I drove the last few miles to work, Dad's words suddenly came back to me as clearly as if he were sitting right there. I recalled that lousy day spent in his machine shop, as well as the physically hard, filthy work that he did six days a week until he finally retired, and as I blinked back the tears I vowed that I would work just as hard in my own life—albeit in a different capacity—to help others escape grinding poverty and neglect.

I always try to keep in mind that, even on my toughest or worst days at work, I still have it better than most people in this world. And when I get stuck on a particularly difficult problem, I often think to myself, "What would Dad do?" before answering, "Work harder!"

I derived help, strength, and loyalty from my family. When I had problems with homework, I turned to my older siblings for help. When I was bored, there was always something going on at our house or someone else to play with. When I needed advice, I had older sisters to help guide me. And when I felt threatened, I had older brothers who were fiercely protective of me. From an early age, the value of family was readily apparent. Still, I never realized as a child that the closeness our parents cultivated would be a tremendous asset when I'd run for political office.

Because my family had been active within our community in so many ways—Little League, Girl Scouts, soccer leagues, church—we had a well established name. Just about everyone knew the Sánchez family personally or had at least heard of us, and this meant that, when I decided to run for Congress, I kicked off my campaign with an army of automatic volunteers. After telling Loretta, I didn't ask the rest of my family for help; I just called and told them where and when to report for duty. Having been through this before, Loretta set a schedule of precinct walking—knocking door-to-door and talking to voters—so that they all had their turn. Including spouses, we had thirteen people standing at the ready to do their part. And this was only the beginning.

Added to the immediate family was our extensive network of cousins, aunts, and uncles who all found ways to pitch in. My aunt Lydia, known for her good cooking, helped Mom make batches of enchiladas, pozole, rice, and beans to feed precinct walkers after a day crisscrossing neighborhoods and talking to voters. One cousin brought his truck, and he and

Dad drove around the district, erecting campaign signs in the yards of people who'd requested them. Two other cousins, who are teachers, organized their colleagues to make phone calls to voters, asking for their support, while Mom's coworkers at the school where she taught clipped press articles about the campaign, as well as about the issues affecting people in my prospective district. It was only thanks to everyone's best efforts that I eventually achieved my goal of becoming a member of Congress.

A couple of weeks after I arrived in Washington, I was on Spanish-language radio, delivering the Democratic rebuttal to the president's State of the Union address. There's a weekly radio show played across a network of Hispanic stations, dealing with whatever issues we've been working on in Congress, and I really appreciated the opportunity to give my impressions on the president's speech, on whether or not I thought he was truly committed to the things he said, and why certain topics were omitted altogether.

Among 435 members of Congress, only 24 are Latino, 3 of them Republican, plus another Republican delegate who can't vote, and that amounts to substantial underrepresentation of America's Hispanic population. One of the problems is, in order to run for Congress you have to raise a lot of money, and Hispanics typically haven't had access to large donors or grown up with wealthy friends who can help them finance their campaigns. Raising enough money to be competitive is usually a huge stumbling block for most minorities. And then there's the infrastructure. Being that we're still underrepresented in both the Democrat and Republican county committees, we don't have the institutional help to launch a campaign if we decide to run.

Then again, when people look at me, I'm not the typical face of who they think of as a member of Congress. They think of older Anglo males, and it can therefore be tough to convince them that a young Latina understands the issues and can do the work as well as someone who's thirty years her senior. People are not accustomed to seeing faces like ours in positions of power, and as such we aren't automatically perceived as candidates who can win.

These days, in Washington, my office is *very* distinguishable from those of other people. The walls are painted bright orange and they're adorned with the works of Latino artists, and there are flowers and throw pillows all around. Anyone who walks in there for the first time wouldn't think it's a member of Congress's office, they'd think it is somebody's living room. It's warm and inviting, and it doesn't have the usual trappings, like a big desk or a "glory wall," featuring all of my awards and photos with famous people. I don't want to impress or overpower anybody. I just want them to feel like I'm inviting them into my home, to sit around a table and chat about whatever's on their minds, and a lot of that goes back to my upbringing.

Everybody was welcome in our house, and while we may not have agreed with all that they said, we were always respectful and hospitable. Again, my home is your home, and that's also how I approach my work—my office is your office. After all, I'm elected by people. They're the ones who hire and fire me, and I'm certainly not better than they are. They're my bosses. They deserve to come in, sit down, and feel welcome, respected, and comfortable when talking to me about the issues that concern them. Beforehand, my staff will offer them drinks and engage them in conversation, and then there's my pet beagle, Chavo, who comes to work with me and is a great little ambassador whenever kids visit. It's a family atmosphere here, and people consistently comment on how much they appreciate that. It reflects how I was raised.

## LORETTA

Our father always taught us by example. He worked hard six days a week providing for us, even though it would be a long stretch to say we were middle class. He taught us to be grateful for our health, our family, and the opportunities we had, and he also never forgot about giving to others less fortunate than we were.

Thanks to Dad working in a rubber-plastics factory, we were always the first kids on the block to have the latest toys: SuperBalls, Hula Hoops, that kind of thing.

And many of those items would also be packed into our Rambler station wagon alongside two suitcases of clothes when all nine of us set off on our annual two-week vacation, visiting family in Mexico. About the third day after arriving to see our grandmother and aunts, Dad would drive us and the toys up into the mountains and stop at small pueblos along the way. In each place, he would motion to some kid who was hanging around, give him a toy, and tell him to go get his friends, and within minutes we'd see scores of kids emerging from little adobe homes, eager for toys. Their eyes would light up as we'd hand out the loot, and the joy on their faces and in their voices was easily matched by what we felt just by giving, let alone sometimes showing them how to actually play with the toys.

My most vivid memory of our parents, as far back as I can remember, is that they worked *really hard*. Mom cooked three meals a day, washed the dishes, cleaned the house, did the laundry, sewed our clothes, and orchestrated our "social calendar." Dad, for his part, would return home from the factory and, no matter how much he washed his hands, the soot of the rubber was always in the lines of his palms. This was a man who knew the value of everybody's contribution.

Once, when I was nine years old and telling him about my day's activities, I rolled my eyes and disparaged a friend by saying, "His dad's just a barber." Dad's eyes flashed and I immediately knew I'd screwed up. Sitting me down, with a stern look on his face, he solemnly explained how *every* job is important, and that you can be proud of whatever you do for a living as long as you're honest and give 100 percent effort every day. He asked me to consider what life would be like if our trash wasn't collected twice a week or if the station attendant didn't help gas up the car.

"Oh, and by the way," he added, "your mother's father was a barber."

Lesson learned. To this day, I honor hard work, and my staff members are always amazed that I know the names of the janitors in our buildings, the Capitol police who protect us, and the women who make my caffe latte each and every morning. I appreciate how hard they work and I'm grateful they're around to enrich my life.

When I was a child, regardless of how poor we were, we'd always get together with family and celebrate. Birthdays, job promotions, recuperations from illness, my uncle's new car, summer...whatever it was, we needed no excuse to celebrate. The women would cook, and then we'd play music and everyone would dance. One of the most beautiful sights I witnessed was of Dad's own mom, well into her eighties, dancing at all the fiestas. In fact, she'd actually start the dancing and then be the last one standing. When we buried Grandma, we had a rosary one night and brought in mariachi to play. We knew she'd want us to celebrate her passing. As a fourteen-year-old, I sat at the rosary and just knew she was dancing in heaven.

Then there was our maternal grandmother, who instilled within our mother the importance of God. I'm glad Mom also did that for me. While Grandma was a devout Catholic — she had an altar in her home with candles and all the saints — our Mom was extremely tolerant of all religions. She not only took us to church on Sunday and enrolled us in Catechism, but she also let us attend other types of church service with our friends. Always convinced that we could get closer to God, she would enroll us each summer in Booster Bible School at the local Church of Christ. However, when we hit our teens, she didn't insist that we go to church. Instead, she told us we could now choose whether or not to believe in God and religion. And the outcome was that we did all continue going to church, even if some of our peers considered this *uncool.*

Teaching us that the Almighty comes in many ways, Mom planted in us a love of God that has served as the cornerstone of my life and helped me make it through the most trying times. And added to this has been the love of *la familia,* whose value is immeasurable within the Hispanic community and which, I believe, will eventually infuse and invigorate the American landscape. We'll reeducate America about the meaning of family.

During my first election campaign against Bob Dornan, few people thought I could win, yet there was no way my parents, eighty-two-year-old grandmother, four brothers, two sisters, and their spouses wouldn't all pitch in to help. They were my volunteer force and fund-raisers. Grandma worked her church group, Mom worked the education community, Dad worked the local business owners, and my brother Iggy convinced his sales force to spend one night a week making ID calls to voters, enticing them with pizza and beer. These were great salespeople and they secured me many votes. Meanwhile, my brother Mike—the single guy in the family—rounded up his friends for Saturday walks and devised games to keep them competitive, so they would register voters and get vote commitments. It really was a collaborative effort.

Then, a month before the election, we received word that President Clinton would be visiting our town to campaign for me, and that I could have a small group of ten people meet the nation's leader and have a photo taken with him. The race with Bob Dornan was now running neck and neck, and since we were short on money for the home stretch, my campaign chairman, Wylie Aitken, wanted to use these ten photo-opportunity slots to raise funds. I told him if there were ten slots, nine must go to my family. The other one could be used to raise money. Furious, he slammed down the phone. I called him back.

"If we don't raise more money, you won't *have* a campaign," he argued.

That year, 1996, the Democratic theme was "Families First."

"I thought this was the 'Families First' president," I replied. "When he comes to town, I want my family to meet him. Win or lose, they've worked so hard for me. No price can be put on all they have done."

That ended the argument. The night before President Clinton's appearance, my chairman sent Paul Goldberg, a friend who knew the president, to ask him for more slots because of my family, and much to the annoyance of his handlers, he agreed. The next day, he and I campaigned in front of twenty thousand people, and then my entire family met the president along with twenty-two other "friends" of—i.e., donors to—the campaign. Family values? We Latinos truly *value* family. But that doesn't mean we sacrifice our personal judgment and thought just to please a crowd.

After Dad decided we should move from El Monte to Anaheim, he and Mom asked our aunts and uncles to join us, but they wanted to stay put. Years later, our cousins then told us their parents subsequently admitted that was the wrong decision. You see, in Orange County we had greater access to a much larger world—the neighborhood was better, there was less congestion, the schools were up to grade, and although initially it wasn't easy being the only Mexicans on the block, we needed to get out of our comfort zone. Our parents weren't trying to escape the Hispanic community; they just wanted a fresh start in a better place for us to grow up, and so they basically took a gamble in the sense that it was a real stretch for them to buy a home there and leave the family behind.

Up until that point, my friends consisted mainly of my cousins. Having to move away from them taught me that, while family's very important, you must also know when to say, "I need to move on." After all, change is always difficult, especially from the known to the unknown, and my aunts and uncles felt more comfortable where they were. While Mom and Dad would have liked all of us to stick together, they weren't going to be dissuaded from pursuing a better life.

As things turned out, that life did prove to be beneficial for us kids, but it wasn't without its stress. For one thing, there was peer pressure to conform to the non-Hispanic community, and in my case this resulted in my becoming anorexic at age sixteen and staying that way for eleven years. The girls I went to school with, sat next to in class, and competed against on the track field were all very thin. And while I certainly wasn't fat, I did have a curvy Mexican body.

Added to that, as a baby I was pudgy, and since it's traditional for Mexican families to give kids nicknames, mine was Gordis, which means fatty. Now, in the American culture, fatty is bad, whereas in the Mexican culture fat babies are good — that's where the two cultures collided. I was stuck with Gordis into high school, and by then I was convinced I really was fat. That's what I saw when I looked in the mirror: fat. So I had to lose weight, I had to run, I had to compete, or else nobody would want to look at me, let alone date me. I couldn't possibly be worth anything unless I was thin. And that's what started my descent into bulimia.

I basically stopped eating and quickly dropped thirty pounds, at which point my Mom and Dad got involved. While Mom kept saying, "She's got to eat," Dad brought his belt to the table, which meant he'd beat me if I didn't comply, and so I'd force the food down and then, without his knowledge, go to the bathroom and purge it all out. He thought he was helping me by administering his version of tough love, without realizing he was dealing with a real mixed-up kid. He would say things like, "You have to realize that you're Mexican. You do not have the same genes as the other girls. You have the genes that are inherent to our people. We're rounder, we're barrel-chested because of the high altitudes in Mexico, and it's not good for you to get skinny."

The problem was, *I* didn't think I was skinny, and I also didn't think I was starving myself. Consequently, by the time I was in college I'd become so thin that, without my knowledge, a roommate called Dad and told him, "You've got to come get your daughter. She hasn't been out of bed for three days, she won't eat a thing, she's anorexic, and you need to save her." The next thing I knew, Dad was coming into my bedroom to take me to the hospital, and I was screaming at my girlfriend, saying, "Why would you do this? How could you betray me?"

I was twenty at the time and not ready to confront my problem. Accordingly, the intervention didn't work and I continued to starve myself for another seven years, until one day I woke up and realized I was on a suicide mission. Finally, I accepted that I'm Latina and that it's okay to not be wafer-thin. I'd never rejected being Mexican — I had a real sense from my parents that this was a good thing. However, with one foot in each culture, I'd been trying to fit into the new one while bringing baggage from the old, and it took me a long time to figure that out. Thankfully I had a loving family to support me while I got the help I needed.

The conflict I'd experienced was self-inflicted. No

one had forced it on me. Sure, like Linda, I had a fair complexion, but my girlfriends knew I was Mexican and they would be the first ones to stand up for me in the face of any racism. I remember several of us lounging by a pool in Palm Springs when I was seventeen or eighteen, and two guys trying to make conversation and laughing about the Mexican pool cleaner. My girlfriends all looked at each other, and then they said, "You know, you're talking to the wrong people. Our girlfriend here — she's Mexican, so get lost." I sort of had them trained that it was okay to be Mexican. After all, *I* was okay.

To this day, the majority of Congress members — even on the Democratic side — don't really get the Latino culture or perspective. They don't understand it; they don't know what makes us tick. And it's really interesting, because so many of them want to learn Spanish and are taking lessons in the mornings. It's like, "Okay, if I learn Spanish, when I campaign I'll be able to demonstrate that I care about them." Well, it's certainly a step in the right direction — Spanish is certainly a common bond among Hispanics, regardless of country. However, I also know many are doing it in order to keep their jobs, not because the language is beautiful and it might enable them to better understand the people and the culture.

In fact, it's not even about liking the culture, because if they liked the culture they would be much more concerned about what's going on in Latin America. Nor would half of them make claims like "Immigrants are bad"—meaning Mexicans in this immigration battle—"so let's get rid of all of them." If they really understood and cared about Hispanic families, they wouldn't allow laws on the books that state "This child is American born—he can stay here. But this mother has no proof of work to be in this country—deport her."

Of course, immigration is a hot topic right now among my colleagues, many of whom are saying the illegal ones are bad for our nation and we've got to get them out of this country. It's up to the likes of Linda and me to tell these members that we're dealing with families, not concepts. We need to educate our colleagues, because if we don't educate them, nobody else in the Congress will do so.

It's certainly true that the people at the forefront of fighting for immigrants' rights have usually come out of the Hispanic Caucus, despite the fact that other groups also have their own undocumented immigrants living in this country. However, just because I'm Latina doesn't mean all Hispanics support me. I'm criticized by Latinos who feel I'm still not standing up for their rights. I hear things like "You don't want enough for us," "You're selling out," "What have you done for us lately?" and "Why can't you get this done?"

Congress is an area of compromise. You are never going to get 100 percent of what you want, so you have to figure out what you'll settle for in terms of your own wants and those of the opposition in order to ultimately help your community. You have to do that same calculation with every substantive issue where you see opposition groups forming, whether you're working with the defense community, the health care community, whomever. And this applies to issues that affect the majority of Hispanics too, yet many Hispanic groups want us to take the all-or-nothing appoach. Truthfully, if we do that we'll probably end up with nothing. That's the reality of Congress.

I am probably the most recognizable Latina on the national political scene, and so people in the Latino community place a lot of expectations on me. It's interesting because I represent an area that, in terms of its voter base, is not predominantly Hispanic. In fact, I'm the only Hispanic in the Congress who doesn't have a Hispanic voting district, per se. Linda has a predominantly Hispanic voting constituency, and so she can be more forthright when it comes to fighting for Hispanic rights, but that doesn't mean I'm not fighting for Hispanic rights, too. It just means I have to fight for these rights because it makes sense for all Americans. Also, since I align myself with the conservative Democrats in the Congress, my job is largely behind the scenes, trying to move the conservative votes to our side. That takes a lot of work that isn't seen. So, when people say to me, "You are the Latina spokesperson, you should be talking on television," I point out that sometimes it's the background activity that will get you over the goal line, not the screaming and yelling.

That having been said, nothing makes me feel more Latina than knowing and using Spanish. When I was young, Dad had me read Spanish literature because he wanted me to love his native tongue the way he did. And when I was a little older, he made sure I took Spanish classes in middle and high school. Since I was a Sánchez, many of the kids would question why I was taking Spanish. They didn't grasp that my dad wanted me to learn the language properly and genuinely enjoy using it. And, *boy,* have I used it.

Typically, when members of Congress—even Hispanic ones—go to Spanish-speaking countries, translators are used. When I went on a ten-day South American tour as part of my work for the Armed Services Committee, there were no translators. The officials of my host countries, and especially all the foreign generals and admirals, loved the fact they could speak to me directly. One of them commented, "You need to get more members in the Congress who understand and speak Spanish like you." I assured him that every day I hear from another colleague who's learning Spanish. It's just a matter of time before many in America will be using English and Spanish. And then Americans will truly know the brilliance of Latin American writers such as Pablo Neruda and Gabriel García Márquez.

The best thing about being Latina is the joy it brings

to my life. Most of my friends and acquaintances know me by my laugh. They'll hear it in a theater and say, "Hey, that must be Loretta." Usually they're right. Joy is all around us. It's in the sounds we hear, it's in the pureness of silence. It's in black and white, it's in color. And it's so evident in little children. We need to remember what it's like to be a child and then return to that joy.

# 3

## Never Say Never

We've frequently been warned – sometimes by well-meaning friends and colleagues – about setting ourselves up for failure by venturing into uncharted territory and biting off more than we can chew. If we listened to these naysayers, our track records wouldn't include Linda's becoming the first Latina head of a union council, Loretta's prying Bob Dornan out of the congressional seat he held with an iron grip for eighteen years, or the two of us being the first sisters in Congress. For that matter, if we had settled for what we were advised was attainable, we would never have gotten college degrees, much less a JD and an MBA, respectively.

The first step toward making anything happen

is to believe it's possible and to have the strength to ignore the noise created by the omnipresent chorus of pessimists...especially if one of those pessimists is inside your own head!

## LORETTA

When I was growing up, one of my dad's favorite sayings was "Don't let anybody ever tell you you're a dumb Mexican." At the time I didn't think about it, but he must have heard that a lot as an immigrant, especially given how Hispanics had been treated in California. He wanted to ensure that his kids would understand they could do whatever they wanted to do with their lives, and that was a recurring theme throughout my childhood.

I remember being in the third grade at Sunkist Elementary School in Anaheim. There were probably thirty kids in our class, and we had these brand-new textbooks about the history of the United States and the local area. The teacher went through the first three chapters, randomly assigned each of us two pages, and told us we had to do projects based on the content of the pages we were given. In my case, this didn't amount to a whole lot, and so I sat and I suffered, unable to figure out what kind of project I could create around these two pages. When I arrived home, I just went to my room and cried, and finally my mother asked me what was wrong.

I said, "Oh, Mom, I've got to do this project that's supposed to take four weeks. It's going to count for half the grade in our class, but it's based on these two pages and there's just nothing in there."

My mom called my dad in, sat him down, and told him what the problem was, and after reading the pages with me they identified two or three things that I could do. These related to just a few words or short phrases, but both of them thought outside of the box, and I was astounded, particularly at my mom. At that time, she didn't speak or read much English, and so for her to go through a couple of pages and suggest ideas was a real eye-opener. Even at age eight, I'd been used to helping my mom and my dad fit into the Anglo world, and yet here they were, teaching me to never defeat myself.

One part of the text mentioned the post office, and my dad said, "Did you notice that we have a new post office down the street?" We'd actually seen it being constructed. "I'll tell you what we could do," he continued. "We could make a replica! It's something to be very proud of in our city, and it's on our side of town. Everyone's really excited about it." Before long, so was I. Dad got me into the station wagon, drove a couple of blocks to the post office's new Sunkist branch, and then used a tape measure, pen, and paper to show me how to draw everything to scale, down to the finest detail. We spent the entire afternoon and evening working on this, and we returned there every day for the next ten days, not only getting all of the dimensions right but also going inside the post office to see how everything was set up.

After showing me how to measure, calculate ratios, and draw accurately, Dad also involved my brothers and sisters in the learning process, getting them to cut the cardboard for my model and select toy cars for the parking lot. It was a lot of fun. However, he also made sure that I did the bulk of the work. The result was an exact replica, I was a big hit at school, and for me that was an important lesson: if you defeat yourself, nothing will get done. But, if you remain calm, look at every possibility, and work with other people, you're sure to come up with a solution.

Since they had suffered discrimination, the last thing our parents wanted was for us to experience that, too. They always told us that, if we studied, the sky was the limit in terms of what we could achieve in this nation. And it was really interesting, because in a sense they even sheltered us from the discrimination that existed in Anaheim. For example, it wasn't until many, many years later that a friend from the other side of the city told me there was a public pool. Mexicans could swim in it only on certain days, and immediately afterward the water had to be changed, but I didn't know that because, instead of telling us about the pool in Anaheim, our father installed one in our backyard. That way, we'd avoid the bigotry.

Our mother made the rule that at home we'd speak Spanish and outside the home we would speak English. Every week, our father assigned us a Spanish-language chapter from something like *Don Quixote,* and on Fridays after work he'd sit down with each of us individually and ask for a report on what we'd read. Our parents wanted us to know about both cultures. To a large extent they understood the importance of our being more American than Mexican, but they also wanted us to value the culture of their home country. Sometimes that was difficult. As the eldest daughter, I went to school, I came home, and that's the way it was. There was no reason for me to go watch the football game against another high school on a Friday night—that, as far as my parents were concerned, was trouble waiting to happen. Never mind that I was in the band that always played at those games. I had to be home, and that was that. It wasn't easy to take. I had a foot in each world, and I learned to navigate them, but things were quite different for my younger siblings.

When I was in graduate school, I came home one time and nobody was there. Wouldn't you know, it was a Friday night, and when my parents finally returned and I asked where they'd been, Mom said, "Oh, we've been at your brother's football game." I said, *"What?"* and she said, "Yes, he's on the football team and we're in the booster club!" I couldn't believe it. I just looked at them and said, "You wouldn't even let me *go* to the football game when I was in high school." My mom got tears in her eyes. "At that time, Loretta, we just didn't know," she said.

It's the same story that plays out with every immigrant family and community. I mean, who goes out and navigates on behalf of the family? Who figures out the school system? Who figures out the Scouts and Little League? My mother was the one who actually did that, and it's only because of her that we got into Bobby Sox Softball and soccer and Little League. That was pretty amazing, because none of those kids' activities were in our parents' Mexican upbringing.

Mom and Dad lacked education because each of their fathers died young, while Mom and Dad were still children, and so they'd never had the opportunities that we enjoyed. However, they were smart, and they always tried to instill in their kids the ability to do those things that they didn't have the chance to do. And that's the case with a lot of immigrants. They work really, really hard and make sacrifices so that the next generation won't have to make those same sacrifices.

My dad was such a great guy when it came to teaching us lessons. I remember, for example, when I learned *why you shouldn't lie.* The house where we lived was next to an alley, and if we walked down there past about ten houses we'd reach the corner of the street, opposite which was Al's Liquor Store. It was like a forerunner of 7-Eleven, and among the items sold there were vegetables. Well, one day around dinnertime, when my mother was making tacos and had forgotten to buy a head of lettuce, she asked my dad to get one at Al's. He'd just arrived home, tired after work, and so he handed a dollar to my older brother, Henry, and asked him to go with me instead. At that time, a head of iceberg lettuce cost 29¢, so after getting one we then decided to buy a couple of candy bars at 5¢ apiece. On the way back, my brother got rid of the lettuce's wrapping, which had the 29¢ tag, and when we arrived home he gave Dad 61¢ change.

When our dad asked for the receipt, Henry told him we hadn't been given one. "Doesn't it come in a plastic wrapper?" Dad asked. "No, it didn't," my brother replied. "It came like this." "Really?" Dad continued. "Are you *sure* this head of lettuce cost thirty-nine cents? That's really expensive."

"Yes, Dad," my brother insisted. "That's what they charged me."

"Are you sure you didn't buy anything extra?"

"Yes, Dad."

One lie followed another, until finally Dad said, "Well, I'll tell you what. We're gonna walk back to Al's, and we'll ask the guy there how much a head of lettuce costs." Now my brother was caught in his web of deceit.

"Okay," he said, "it only cost twenty-nine cents, but we bought a couple of candy bars." That's what our Dad wanted to hear. "It's okay that you bought the candy bars," he said, "but you should be honest about it. You see, it's wrong to lie, because once you set off down that path you're gonna have to use another lie to cover up for it, and then another, and another, and pretty soon you're gonna have a whole string of lies."

That's how Henry and I learned not to lie. And although *we* were questioned, we weren't allowed to question the wisdom of our parents. At least, not at an early age. In fact, even when I was seventeen and about to buy my first car, Dad accompanied me to the dealership. The car I wanted was new off the lot, and with tax and license it cost $3,400. Well, I had saved $2,400, and the dealer said they would lend me the extra $1,000 if my dad would cosign. The interest rate was 8 percent, and I said, "Okay, great." I already had a part-time job that enabled me to do that, but my dad said, "No, no, no, no. I'll lend you the thousand dollars and you can pay me back." That was fine with me, so I drove away in my brand-new car, and when we arrived home Dad drew up a payment schedule and I noticed he was charging me 13 percent interest.

I said, "But, Dad, the dealer was only going to charge me eight percent! Why are you charging me thirteen?" And he said, "Because I want to teach you a lesson, and the lesson is this: you should never borrow, but only buy things when you have the money to do so. That's why I want to make it really hurt you." For him, cash-and-carry was the bottom line, and to this day that's what he does. The only thing for which he's ever taken out a loan is his home. So, I did end up paying him the 13 percent interest, and when I finished doing that after a year I discovered that he'd placed the extra money in a savings account for me. Still, the lesson had been learned, and this kind of thing happened all the time when I was growing up, both inside and outside the home.

At school, all of my teachers were great. One of them, Mrs. Helms, whom I still see once in a while, taught the special classes that I attended in both fifth and sixth grades after having been identified as a "mentally gifted minor" with an IQ over 160. I loved to write, and she always encouraged me in that regard. She was incredibly creative, had a lot of contacts, and would really work hard to get the most out of her students. One time, there was a writing contest on the subject "Why do you want to be police chief for the day in the city of Anaheim?" The winner would get to do just that, and Mrs. Helms told me she wanted me to enter, so I agreed. When the day arrived to submit our essays, I hadn't bothered, and I told her this as if it wasn't such a big deal. Well, she actually pulled me out of class and sent me down to the library, saying, "You will write your essay."

That's exactly what I did, and the result was that I won at both the school and district levels, and became police chief for the day. In fact, I still have this picture of me as a ten-year-old, standing in front of a 1960s Anaheim police car, and when I first ran for Congress that's the photo that appeared on my brochure: "The Anaheim Kid." The point is, my teachers didn't just encourage me, they *made* me do things, and I'm really grateful for that. Sometimes there were teachers who didn't have that kind of faith in me. I was a good student and really excelled at Katella High School, taking the preliminary SAT as a junior and prequalifying as a national merit scholar. When I received invitation letters from the top colleges and sat down to discuss these with a school administrator, his advice was to go to a community college. When I asked why, he replied, "Well, you know, Mexican families don't really want to let their kids out of their sight, and you can get a good education here for the kinds of things you're going to do. That way you can live at home and it won't be expensive."

Whereas Linda's high school would be in a more Hispanic area, mine was in a predominantly Anglo neighborhood. I was one of only a handful of Latinos, and the administrator's perception of us was clear: Mexican families can't afford to send their kids to school. What he didn't appear to consider was that I had great test scores and college representatives saying they wanted to fly me out and have me attend their schools. Again, he had a preconceived notion of what Hispanics were all about. And yet, when I ran into him about five years ago, he told me, "Oh, I'm so proud you. I just knew you were going places." It was like he had no recollection of our earlier conversation.

For me, self-belief was learned over time, and I was fortunate in that, when I was encouraged to try things, I often succeeded. At age twenty-four, I started competitive bike riding, doing fifty miles or one hundred miles and riding every day. It's interesting because when I'd see a big mountain in front of me I'd always think, "I'm never gonna make that," yet I'd take it on and find that it wasn't as hard as I'd imagined. When the terrain in front of me was flat and looked like it would be no problem at all, it would often turn out to be very, very difficult. And that's what bike riding taught me: you can't assume something's going to be easy or difficult. You just have to assume that you're going to last the course. If you prejudge something as being too hard, it sometimes *will* become harder, and so the only thing you should decide is that you're going to do it.

I did very well in my career as a financial advisor, working all over California, and when I moved back to Anaheim and asked my mom what I should do with my spare time, she advised me to go back to my junior high and high schools and help kids learn the skills they would need to become as successful as I was. Accordingly, I became involved with summer school classes and mentoring programs in science and math that really helped change many kids' lives. And it changed my life too. The experience inspired me to then go to the school board members and say, "We need to do this at all the schools here in Anaheim." Their attitude was "We don't want to change things," and even when I talked with Mayor Tom Daly, who was a friend that I'd grown up with, he said, "That's not really within the jurisdiction of what the city does."

I next tried to make an appointment to see my Congress member, Bob Dornan, but he refused to meet with me. If I had said I wanted to meet with him about a defense project, he would have been all over it, but as far as I could tell education held no interest for him. So, at that point I went home and said, "I'm going to run for Congress." In a lot of ways I didn't really know what that meant. I just knew that this guy had made me mad, that if he was going to treat me that way, then he was probably treating other people that way, too, and so he therefore had to go. I was thirty-five years old at the time and I was a Democrat because I wanted things to change in Orange County, and since we didn't have much representation, if anyone was going to get rid of him it would have to be me.

The first person I called was my mom. When I told

her what I wanted to do, she said, "Okay, we can do that." She probably thought it would be like running for the city council. When I told other people about my plan, they pointed out that, in addition to having never raised political campaign funds or held political office, I was also a Latina and a woman, and as such I'd never be elected in Orange County. I heard this not only from the local paper, but also from the Democratic party, which already had its candidate whom I'd have to defeat in the primary. You know, "She's been away at school," "She's not really a part of the community," "She couldn't possibly know what it needs," "She's a carpetbagger," and on and on.

If anybody tells me I can't do something, that's a bad move. And in the case of prying Bob Dornan out of his seat, I would never have tried doing something that I didn't think I had a chance of achieving. As things progressed, I never had moments of doubt about me, but I did have moments of doubt about people who said they would help me and then didn't. Those were the discouraging moments. But, I always thought I could win. Once it was all over my husband told me, "Oh, come on, Loretta, nobody thought you were going to win." I said, "Well, how could that be? You walked door-to-door with me and always seemed to believe," and he said, "Yeah, I'm your husband, I'm supposed to be supportive. But I didn't think you were *going to win*."

That amazed me. I mean, thank God, my husband was

supportive, because I couldn't have won without him, but the thought of losing never really entered my mind. And throughout my time in Congress, even when I've had to battle overwhelming odds, I've learned to never say never. I've sat on the Armed Services Committee right from the start, which makes me the ranking woman (the woman with the most seniority in the House on defense). That means I get calls about many issues, particularly from women in the military who hope I'll have a sympathetic ear. Back in 2004, following a scandal over rapes by military cadets at the Air Force Academy, it emerged that during the previous fifteen years there had been eighteen reports from the Pentagon to Congress describing how to put a stop to all of the sexual assault scandals. Nevertheless, the same offenses had continued to take place. I thought about this for a while and came up with three things that needed to be done regarding this issue.

First, we needed to change the sexual assault law with respect to prosecuting the offenders within the Uniform Code of Military Justice (UCMJ), because it had not been updated since the 1950s to reflect the changes in how rape is now defined. As it was, when these incidents took place within the military, they'd put the women on the stand and go after them for being promiscuous, blame them if they had been drinking because it contravened the code for cadets, and generally abide by the old rules that invariably favored the men. These didn't match the laws that we have for civilians, which were updated by the Congress in 1985 to reflect reality.

The second thing I wanted to do was change the culture. I mean, why do guys perpetrate these acts and, in many cases, feel they have the right to do so? And then the third thing to change was how the victims were treated, since they weren't being provided with the services that would help them cope with their trauma. Having analyzed what needed to be done, I drafted, with a lot of help from a military prosecutor, a revised version of the military law, and then I arranged a dinner meeting with John McHugh, the Republican chairman of the House Committee on Armed Services personnel subcommittee, to explain how this could be put into effect with the cooperation of the Pentagon.

After that, I introduced it as a bill and was visited in my office by several Pentagon lawyers, many of them one-star generals an admirals. I told them that what I'd drafted for the military code was really a mirror of the civilian law that had already been adopted at the federal level and in thirty-seven states, and I remember encountering an attitude of, "Oh, that will never happen. We will never change that law. There hasn't been a major revision to the UCMJ in the last sixty years, and you're not about to do that." You see, they've got this Red Book, about as thick as three Bibles, that serves as the operating manual for prosecutors in the military.

"If we changed the law we would have to change the Red Book," one lawyer remarked. "That would take *forever*, and people would have to relearn how to prosecute these cases."

"Well, how long do you think it would take to revise the Red Book to reflect the changes we want to make to the military code?"

"Oh, at least nine months," his assistant replied.

"Okay," I said, "I'll tell you what I'll do. We'll pass the law today with the provision that it becomes active in nine months. That way, you'll have the time to rewrite your little Red Book."

"Oh no, we couldn't do that. You don't understand the military, Miss Sánchez. Let us walk you through this."

Some of those men were really condescending. I got the distinct feeling that they thought the problem wasn't nearly as bad as I was making it out to be—never mind that eighteen reports in fifteen years was an unacceptable state of affairs. They didn't want anybody meddling with the UCMJ. Any changes to it were normally initiated by the lawyers within the military, and now here was this young woman telling them, "We need to go after these guys, but the existing laws don't help to prosecute them." Their reaction was that it would be *a lot of work* to change things.

I told them, "Every time we change a law in Congress,

prosecutors have to change their way of prosecuting. If we used your logic, we'd never change any laws at all!"

Still, they kept throwing little roadblocks my way— "No, no, it's much more difficult than that"—until finally I said, "Well, gentlemen, I'm going to do this." And I looked at those who'd told me it wasn't going to happen, and I said, "You, obviously, have never been raped. Because if you had been, you would understand the need to change this law." I basically threw the gender issue at them, and then I stood up to signal the meeting was over, adding, "It will be interesting working through this with all of you." I was very civil and very nice, and we parted company in a cordial manner, but after they'd left I thought, "It's going to take me about eight years to get this done."

There had never, ever been a major revision done outside of this lawyer cabal. It was *their* military code of justice, and nobody could know better about it than the military lawyers. What they didn't understand was that many people of lower rank, who were prosecutors within the military, were advising me, providing me information, and telling me what was needed to enable them to put the offenders behind bars. While the lawyers at my meeting knew they had to be nice to the congresswoman, I could tell some were thinking, "Ha, whatever! We're just gonna stonewall this lady and pretty soon she'll forget all about the little hearing that she wants to do."

John McHugh subsequently raised the issue, and he asked the Pentagon to file a report, which would take nine months to compile and a year to deliver, since everything is done in one-year cycles. Well, over the next year the report never materialized, and when Mr. McHugh insisted that it be turned in four weeks after the original deadline, it was clear that it didn't comprise nine months' worth of work, but more like two days'. That made him really mad, and so he then called a hearing at which he began his introductory remarks by saying he was pretty angry at the fact that they hadn't done this report because they obviously didn't think we were serious about it. After eighteen reports submitted in fifteen years, nothing had changed, and despite my working very hard and producing extremely solid information, they had chosen to pooh-pooh me, and then also chosen to pooh-pooh Mr. McHugh by not even doing the report the way he'd asked them to.

"We're now going to mark up Miss Sánchez's proposal," he announced, and that's exactly what happened. The personnel subcommittee allowed it to move forward to the full committee, of which Duncan Hunter was the chairman, and we thought he was going to pull it out. However, Mr. McHugh told him behind closed doors, "I have the votes on our side, and if you put it to a vote, Mr. Hunter, you will lose. This needs to change, Miss Sánchez has done a good job on it, and so this should move forward." In fact, they let it move forward that day, and it ended up being signed by the president in the full Department of Defense bill. That meant the law had been enacted within two years of my starting work on it, and it was the first major revision to that code in over sixty years.

When you first enter the Congress you want to change the world, but you soon learn it's an incremental process. The same topics come up every year—health care, energy, transportation, military issues, you name it—but nothing happens until the time and conditions are right. A lot of it has to do with what the subject is and who controls the Congress, whether or not you're in control, and whether you can work with people on the side, just like I worked with Mr. McHugh. After all, he didn't have to do that. He could have just said, "Nah, I'm not gonna do this. It's not going anywhere, Sánchez," and that would have been the end of it. Instead, he listened to what I had to say and he understood that I was trying to work with him, so he gave me a chance.

I have learned persistence, and I've also learned that the game does not go to the flash in the pan. The game goes to the one who works methodically, just as the tale of the tortoise and the hare applies generally in life. And it's interesting, because when people look at me a lot of them think I'm the flash—"Oh, she's on TV," "Oh, she won an upset victory"—but they don't see the work that

I do behind the scenes, and how trying to get something done in Congress is a very methodical process.

The Democratic Congressional Campaign Committee (DCCC), which tries to get more people elected to the House of Representatives, always try to send as many potential candidates as possible to meet with me. That's because I give them a reality check. I tell them, "You've got to believe in yourself. No one's going to raise money for you. The excitement's got to come from you, and so has the motivation. Don't think all you have to do is smile and take a nice photograph or make a good speech. *You've* got to go door-to-door. *You've* got to raise the money. It comes from you, and you have to be persistent."

You have to keep reality in front of you. Things don't get done by way of a pie-in-the-sky approach. You get something done by looking at the risks and concluding that, although the chances are low, you can still be successful if the moon and stars are in alignment. And if that's the case, you'll be the one who makes it happen.

## LINDA

We grew up in a Latino family where our father was the patriarch. His word was the law, especially for the girls, and our poor mom had to act as the intermediary and our negotiator. Never mind that we were being raised in a country where the culture was more permissive for girls than it was back in Mexico. Dad didn't want to know about that. If an elementary school friend was having a birthday slumber party, he'd be adamant that I couldn't go. "You have a bed here," he'd say. "Why do you need to go sleep at somebody else's house?"

We didn't question our father and we certainly didn't talk back. In fact, when I heard how some of my friends spoke to their parents, I was shocked. In our family we'd have had our teeth knocked out for being so fresh. The only way to appeal one of Dad's decisions was to try to get Mom to soften him up. She'd tell him, "Nacho, this is how girls celebrate birthdays here, and if she doesn't go she'll be considered different to the other kids. Don't worry, she's going to be chaperoned." My father's big thing was we girls being chaperoned. He didn't want us getting into anything crazy, so adult supervision and chaperoning were crucial. In fact, when Loretta started dating, if she wanted to go out with a boy, she had to take me along so "nothing would happen." You can just imagine how much she loved *that*. Being one of the oldest children, she was raised much more strictly than I was—by the time they got to me they were tired. The older kids really broke them in.

It was never easy to sway our father. And as we knew better than to buck authority, I sometimes found it very, very hard not only to speak up for myself, but also to do something beyond that which was expected of me. This was even true when it came to sports, which I loved doing from an early age and which Dad encouraged because he saw them as a great alternative to gangs and drugs: "Keep them busy to keep them out of trouble."

From the age of eight I played soccer in a league outside school, guided by a gruff, heavyset Italian coach named Mr. Smaldino who'd yell instructions at us in a huge, booming voice, and who also taught me how to become more assertive. Having been used to never questioning authority or speaking unless spoken to, I just did what he said and hardly spoke a word. He would say, "Nod your head if you understand what I'm telling you," and so that's what I did. Later I learned that, for the better part of a year, because I was so shy, he didn't know I spoke English! It was only during the second year, when I became friendly with his daughter, who was really mouthy, that I became more vocal, and then no one could stop me. In fact, I remember one day when he was mapping out drills on a chalkboard and I was talking to her about something, he got really mad, threw down the chalkboard, and yelled, "Sánchez, would you shut up while I'm trying to go through this drill? We spent a year trying to get you to speak, and now I can't get you to shut up!"

And even today, despite the requirements of my job, I don't like to be in the media spotlight. I do it because my work necessitates it. Nevertheless, it was as a result of participating in sports as a kid that I learned to be more vocal and assertive—I remember Coach Smaldino once telling us before a game, "Look, you are young ladies when you're off the soccer field. You can talk about boys and nail polish as much as you like. However, when you step onto this field you are not a young lady, you're a soccer player, and that means you must be focused and aggressive." For me that was like getting permission to be competitive, and that in turn really taught me something.

Consequently, when I went to junior high and there wasn't a girls' soccer team, I signed up for the boys' team instead. That created kind of a ruckus, especially as I was joined by a couple of other girls who'd previously played alongside me. They said, "If you try, we'll try," and as it turned out all three of us made the team. Of course, at first the boys weren't happy, and the coach was also a little unprepared for us showing up, but we knew how to play, and play well, and I ended up not only making the team but also the all-star team at the end of the year.

Now fast-forward to my freshman year in Congress, when I found out there was a congressional baseball team. I had played competitive fast-pitch softball, so I showed up for the first practice and I was the only woman there. Well, never mind that I was among Democrats—you know, progressive, open-minded people. Nobody said a thing, yet their looks said it all: "What is she trying to prove? This is hardball, this is baseball." Then, once we had batting practice and they saw that I could hit the ball, there was a whole new level of respect. Of course, after my first hit there was a general sense of "She got lucky," but I'm a very consistent hitter. Since the guy who was pitching had played triple-A ball, it didn't take long for him and everyone else to wise up. I was in the lineup to play the Republicans, and since then I've been the only woman on the Democrat team. Some of my closest colleagues in Congress—Bill Pascrell, Mike Doyle, Tim Bishop, and Bart Stupak—are the guys I play baseball with, and who cheer me on at practice and in the games.

In the 2007 game, we Democrats mustered only five hits, and mine was one of them. The year before, the Democrats had seven hits and mine was one of those, too. Each time I get a hit, even the Republicans cheer! They have a few women who put on the uniform, but they aren't really baseball players. When I've been on the Hill the day after a game, I've had young women staffers approach me and say, "I saw you in the baseball game last night. That was amazing. You're out there, competing with the guys, and you're just as good as they are." That's important to me. I know I'm not the best player on the team, but I'm also not the worst. I just try to contribute to the effort, and I definitely *do* contribute, illustrating that women can compete with men in any career, any field.

From the start I was raised according to traditional gender roles and an Old Country mentality. Yet, as time went on, Mom—who went back to school and graduated from college—became more open-minded and understanding of the culture we were living in. She realized this was not Mexico and that kids do things a little bit differently here. This coincided with me becoming more rebellious, constantly asking her "Why?" in terms of how my brothers were treated. Okay, so

I was used to always eating in shifts—with Dad and the boys invariably going first—because we had a small kitchen table. But as I grew older and, thanks to my sporting experiences, a little more confident, I began complaining about how the guys were allowed to go out, stay up later, and have fewer chores. They had a lot more liberty and a lot less responsibility than the girls. And they also had more privileges.

My soccer coach, Mr. Smaldino, had two kids, and when his son turned sixteen, he got a car: a beat-up Bug, but a car. Then, when his daughter turned sixteen, she got a car, too. There was equality in their family that I didn't see in mine. I was always asking Mom, "Why do the boys get to do that and we don't?" and "Why do we have to be the ones to clean the house and do extra chores if we want to go out, but they only have to mow the lawn once a week?" Most times she'd say, "Well, that's just the way it is and you've got to deal with it," but then there also was the day when she remarked, "If you don't like it, go to law school and change it." I was about eleven years old, and that's the moment when a light went on in my head—Hey, there *is* a way to make things fairer!

Of course, I could push my mother's buttons, but if I'd done that with my dad he would have packed me up and sent me to a convent in some hamlet in Mexico, and nobody would have ever heard from me again. I'm not kidding—if any of us girls weren't doing well at school or focusing too much on boys, that was his big threat: "I could take you to a village in Mexico where they don't have telephones or even electricity...You'd better straighten up or you're gonna find yourself in a town where there are no cars, only horses."

There was no equality between the boys and girls, and there sure wasn't between Mom and Dad, either. That's why, when I played on the soccer team, it was so great to compete with boys and show them that "I can do what you can do, and even do it better than some of you." However, while there were very clear gender roles, I have to say the one area where those didn't exist was education. Both of our parents always pushed their daughters to do well at school and wanted us to have careers, and in that respect our dad was way ahead of his generation. He believed that not only the boys should go to college, but that the girls should go there, too. The immigrant experience had resulted in his wanting a better life for his kids, and he knew the way to move up was through education.

We had relatives who'd tell me, "Go work in a bank so you can meet a rich man," or "Go work in a clothing store so you can get a discount on what you wear." To them, a job like that was good enough for a girl. But Mom and Dad would tell me to ignore what they said. And they'd also take their own advice when people would ask, "Why do you want your kids to go to college? Have them get a job and help support the family." My parents were like, "No. When they graduate from college they're going to have a lot more choices and earn a lot more money."

This certainly refuted the theory of one of my high

school teachers, who once started a lesson in government and politics by declaring there should be separate schools for black students, separate schools for Asian students, and separate schools for Mexican students. When I challenged him on this, saying I found it really offensive, he replied, "Well, look at the dropout rates for Mexican girls. There's no need for them to go to college. They're just going to get pregnant and drop out anyway."

It was 1987, and there were three minority students in that class of thirty-eight: me, another Latina named Miriam, and an Asian student named Daniel, whom I also felt bad for—when referring to Asians, our teacher actually called them "Ornamental" instead of Oriental, as if that term weren't already inappropriate. He obviously thought that was cute, but to me it was humiliating and I knew it was wrong. We just had to soak it up while no one else said a thing. At that age I wasn't too articulate, but I still voiced my objections. I cut class the next day because being a part of it felt so wrong. As a result, I was hauled into the vice principal's office, and when he questioned me about my absence I told him, "Look, I'm not going back until the teacher apologizes."

The vice principal suggested the teacher was playing devil's advocate to spark a discussion.

"Well, it didn't seem that way," I replied. "He was being hurtful, we were outnumbered, and since nobody stood up to defend us, we had to defend ourselves. It was as if all the other students agreed with him . . . I'm not going back."

"Yes you are," he said. "Otherwise, you'll be suspended."

When I told my mom what had happened, she was adamant: "You will absolutely not go back to that class." She, too, was offended. So, she called the principal, and in the end, instead of arranging a showdown where the teacher would have to apologize, the school simply transferred me to a different classroom with a different teacher.

I had experienced racism before, but in a unique sort of way. Because I was a blonde-haired kid, people would say derogatory things to me about Mexican people while assuming I wasn't one of them, and I would get really mad: "Uh, excuse me, my last name is Sánchez." Still, even after I said that, they wouldn't have the decency to be embarrassed and say, "Oh, I'm so sorry!" Instead, they'd just say, "Oh, but *you're* different." Yeah, that's right: I'm the only one who's different, and all the rest are riffraff—how simpleminded and insulting!

I grew up hearing stuff like that, yet when my teacher went into his racist diatribe, categorizing minorities and asserting that Mexican girls who went to college would probably just "get pregnant and drop out anyway," I was more than annoyed and insulted. His statement lodged itself inside my head and served to make me more determined than ever to prove him—and others like him—wrong. Sure, there were times during my childhood when, having been told I wasn't capable of doing something, I'd feel dispirited and think, "I'm obviously not smart enough to do that." But as the years went on and I gained a greater sense of myself through success in sports and academic achievements, discouraging comments began to have the reverse effect on me—tell me I couldn't do it and I'd only want to do it more.

In high school I had a friend named Danielle. She was one of very few black students in our freshman year, and she really stood up for herself. She didn't let people walk all over her or push her around, and to a certain extent I learned that from her—"I'm not going to defer to you." In fact, at one point my mom actually thought she was a bad influence on me, especially when I kept harassing her about the boys getting away with more than the girls. She didn't like that feistiness. But, hey, what's not to like? From very early on, I was always the kid who stuck up for the underdog, and when one of my teachers said, "You have the makings of an attorney," that idea appealed to me.

I never actually thought I would serve in elected office. That was not something I set out to do, even though it was really inspiring to see Loretta upset the odds by getting elected to Congress on her first attempt, especially since she defeated the eighteen-year incumbent, who had previously run for president and who proved to be a very nasty opponent. Instead, after graduating from UCLA law school in 1995, I got a job working at a small law firm. I was the only female attorney there, but initially I didn't think about that. I dealt with cases that involved employment and gender discrimination until one day a partner refused to consider hiring a pretty secretary simply because her looks might distract the guys—guys who were handling *discrimination* cases!

I never really felt like they treated me as an equal, but when I complained to Loretta about the good ol' boy network in that office, she laughed and said, "Linda, don't complain to me. I'm working in the *ultimate* good ol' boy network up here in Washington, D.C.!" They were still trying to keep her from being seated as a member of Congress because she'd won her election by such a tight margin. However bad it was for me, Loretta had it worse. So, I decided to suck it up, until Paul Rich, an electricians union leader whom I met while helping with Loretta's 1997 reelection campaign, encouraged me to apply for a job with the International Brotherhood of Electrical Workers (IBEW). So I took Paul's advice and applied for a position ensuring that construction workers on tax-payer-funded public works projects were being paid the prevailing wage.

The Central Labor Council (CLC) of Orange County, which is the umbrella organization for all of the county's unions, had fairly weak leadership at that time, and people kept telling me they wanted to elect someone more dynamic to run it. I was part of a group looking at whom we could recruit to do that, and when those whom we approached weren't able to accept, the spotlight turned on me. Initially, I was hesitant, because labor was a big supporter of Loretta, and I didn't want to create factions that supported different candidates and have them take it out on her. So, the committee told her they wanted me to run for the position, and when Loretta saw I had plenty of support, she said, "Well, I'm not about to discourage her from doing it."

That's when I decided to run, and at that point I absolutely believed I could be successful. I knew that, with hard work and a good strategy, I'd probably win, and that things would be better under fresh leadership. A few people on the executive board were among the naysayers who thought I was too young and inexperienced in union matters, but I ended up winning the election, and as such I became the first minority woman in the U.S. to head a Central Labor Council. One of my first tasks was to help organize the janitors in Orange County, a task many people told me could never be accomplished. Well, not only did we organize them, but we also got them their first contract, all within nine months. It was a very quick campaign and it was very successful.

The other big campaign that we took on was on behalf of the in-home care workers who are paid by the county to help elderly and disabled people cook, clean, bathe, and dress themselves. These people, who provide such essential care for those with health problems, didn't even have health care benefits. So, we launched a campaign for better wages and health care benefits and that, too, was ultimately successful. As a result, I learned early in my career to ignore all of the negative voices: "Oh, it's way too difficult. You'll never do it." Wanna bet?

Each successive experience helped build my confidence. As I always tell people—and I really believe this—I'm not the smartest kid in the room, but I can work incredibly hard and I can be incredibly focused. Early on in life, I did think you had to be the smartest person in order to go to law school or get an internship in Washington, D.C. But as I grew older and managed to deal with some really big challenges, I started to understand that the only real limitations came from myself. There will always be naysayers who'll try to sabotage you, either because they don't want to see you succeed or because they're jealous, or simply because they don't want to do the work that you're willing to do. In my case, I never ask anybody in the office to do something that I wouldn't do myself. And these are people who work *with* me, not *for* me, because I regard whatever we do as a team effort.

I loved my labor job. However, in 2000 there was a census, followed by a re-districting of congressional, state assembly, and state senate seats. Because California's population had grown, an additional congressional seat was created where I lived. At first, this didn't make an impact on me because I never thought I would run for office. But things started to change when I saw that the Democratic heir apparent to the seat was an elderly woman who'd served the maximum number of terms in the State Assembly, and who, in my mind, was very lukewarm on issues such as choice and labor rights; all the things that I'd spent my life fighting for.

Because her assembly district contained four of the ten

cities in the new congressional district, everyone said she was the front-runner to represent that seat, but I couldn't believe she was the best candidate the Democrats could come up with. I was married at that time, and I kept telling my husband, Mark, "This is terrible, she's not going to be a passionate advocate for this district," until finally one day he said, "Look, Linda, instead of just complaining about it, why don't you do something?" What I think he meant was "Why don't you find someone better to run?" but it made me think: "Well, I know the issues—I've worked on a lot of them; I've run a field campaign for Loretta; she is very good at raising money...Do I think I could do a better job than that woman? Absolutely!" So I decided to run.

The next day I informed Loretta of my decision, and the day after that she agreed to help while also asserting that we needed to move fast because she'd heard other candidates were making the rounds in D.C. That's when I learned that the young Latino mayor of South Gate, the largest city in my district, had been in Washington, trying to court support. So, we worked very quickly, and from then on I was totally committed. Not that it was easy—in total, there were five other Democratic candidates in the primary, and immediately some community activists told me, "You're too young, Linda, wait your turn," and, best of all, "You should run for the school board. Women care about education."

I'd hear this at meetings where I was trying to gather support, and occasionally from local leaders in one-on-one discussions. Some of it may have been well intentioned, but without a doubt the "advice" of certain individuals was downright patronizing. The mayor was the same age as I was, and, yes, unlike me, he'd held elected office at the local level. But he was also a man, and I'm sure that helped him. After all, aren't men the ones who run for Congress while women run just for the school board?

These comments came more from men than from women, but when I was informed that the new congressional district was "the mayor's seat" I responded, "You know whose seat that is? That seat belongs to whoever can win it and hold on to it, and that's gonna be me."

I announced my candidacy in August 2001, and as things progressed the voices against me only grew more vociferous, especially once I became the front-runner courtesy of more endorsements and the most money raised. Not only did I have plenty of meetings with Washington's base Democratic groups, but Loretta really worked on her colleagues to help me, and by the end of the year the other five candidates were all attacking me in debates and in the press. It got very ugly.

For instance, we attended an editorial board meeting with the *Long Beach Press-Telegram* where all the candidates came in to pitch why they should be endorsed by the newspaper. Instead of us being interviewed one-on-one, they had us all in the room at the same time—a solid journalistic ploy for maximum conflict. We each had two minutes to deliver an opening statement as to why we thought we should represent the district, and then the candidates were allowed to grill one another. Well, guess who was the center of attention. I immediately had five people jumping all over me, making all kinds of allegations. It turned into a free-for-all.

One of the candidates accused me of having had four addresses without ever living in the district. *Wrong.* I'd bought my home in 1999, prior to the census that had led to the redistricting, so there was no way I could have known it would be in a new district. I tried to remain calm and unruffled while five people were shouting at me, making all these allegations. I told them, "Look, I'll address each issue one by one, but I can't answer you all when you're yelling at me at the same time. Are you even interested in what I have to say, or are you more interested in making allegations and yelling at me?"

I stayed in the meeting to try to address some of the more egregious accusations, but after about an hour I left for another meeting and the press wrote some really nasty things about me. It was hard. At the last primary debate, one of the other candidates pounced on the fact that my married name was Linda Sánchez-Valentine. Never mind that everybody knew me professionally as Linda Sánchez. I had practiced law as Linda Sánchez and been elected to the Labor Council as Linda Sánchez, so when I ran for Congress I used the name Linda Sánchez. Well, now an African American man was alleging that I wasn't really Hispanic, and that I had changed my name to pander to the Hispanic vote! My mom, an immigrant from Mexico, was in the audience, and after listening to his accusation she got up and exclaimed, "You don't even know what you're talking about!"

It's kind of embarassing when your mom is defending you in a debate, but she got really upset. That is the thing that's hardest—as a candidate you learn to develop a really thick skin, but the family gets hurt, and usually it's over things that have been made up out of thin air. Obviously, when people attacked me my first reaction was to defend myself, and then, when I thought about it a little more, I'd get angry at some of the ridiculous things being said, but sometimes I'd also feel beaten down. I remember returning home after a fourteen-hour day of campaigning, hearing terrible slurs against me in public, and reading half-truths about me in the press, and feeling so low that I questioned if this was even worth it. My husband, who was very supportive of the campaign, said, "Linda, you're the front-runner, everybody's trying to tear you down. You're doing a great job. Hang in there. Tomorrow's gonna be better."

Just those few words of encouragement really made a difference. I got up the next day thinking, "Okay, I'm ready to do battle." Self-belief was never very far away, and over the course of fifteen months, from winning the primary until I was elected to Congress in November 2002, it only got stronger. Initially, I was shocked by the vehemence of all the bile being hurled at me, but eventually I became battle-hardened and increasingly determined, especially when polling indicated that my support was fairly consistent.

Still, when it came to Election Day I did get a little nervous. A very good friend of mine from the labor movement, who'd been on board with me right from the start, called ten days before the primary election. He had stuck his neck out, supporting me over the other candidates, and now he sounded really panicked. Point-blank, he asked me, "Linda, can you win this race?" I replied, "Adam, I *am* going to win." His ass was on the line and I was concerned that he didn't have the faith, but I knew—I knew—I was going to win the race.

Growing up, I'd felt more unequal being a girl than being Latino, not least because of the gender roles that were reinforced at home. When some of my colleagues were dismissive of me during my first couple of years in Congress, I couldn't tell if this was because I'm a woman, because I'm Latino, or because I was young, elected at age thirty-three. It could have any or all of those factors, but I could hardly ask, "Excuse me, did you just blow me off because I'm a woman, because I'm Hispanic, or because I'm young? Could you let me know?" Instead, I just had to suck it up and stand firm.

Like everyone else, when I first came up to the Hill and was going through orientation I immediately began lobbying members of Congress for my committee assignment. I desperately wanted to be on the Judiciary Committee, because it deals with constitutional law, civil rights, immigration, and many more areas that I find fascinating. There were also more senior members vying for a slot on that committee, and since Democrats were then in the minority and committee assignments were really hard to get, a more senior colleague from California told me, "Linda, you'll be lucky if you get on the *Agriculture Committee*." I told him I didn't think Agriculture would be a very good fit for my district, which was urban/suburban. "Precisely. You'll be lucky if you get on Agriculture."

Well, I was determined—I was going to find some way of getting on the Judiciary Committee. I lobbied the members who sat on the steering committee, as well as the office of the leader, Nancy Pelosi, and enlisted Loretta's help as well. It was kind of interesting—there were no actual openings on the committee, because every member who'd been on there the year before had been reelected. So, there I was, having spent all this time lobbying for a nonexistent slot, feeling really panicked and scrambling around to figure out what other committees I might try to aim for.

Then I received word that Barney Frank, a senior member from Massachusetts who'd sat on the Judiciary Committee, had just vacated his position to take over the minority leadership role on Financial Services. That meant Judiciary had one slot, and I was vying with members who'd been in Congress for two or three terms. Well, January 28, 2003, was the date of the State of the Union address, and it was also my birthday, and I received a call from Rosa DeLauro, one of the leader's go-to persons, that I'd landed the slot on the Judiciary Committee!

The fact that our leader was a woman probably helped put me over the top, as did the lack of any Hispanics, either Democrat or Republican, on that committee. Don't forget, it deals with immigration, and I'm sure it's because the majority leader saw the need for diversity that she jumped me ahead of two or three people who'd been waiting a long time to get on there. The odds of me edging out the competition had been slim-to-none. So, once again I'd learned: *never say never.*

Washington is a very competitive place, but I'm not a hell-driven, ambitious, cutthroat, stab-my-mother-in-the-eye-to-get-what-I-want member of Congress. I'm a team player, the one who tries to work with everybody, the one who is reasonable and can compromise. My personal ambition is never more important than the agenda we're advancing. For plenty of people here it *is* all about them first. The more unreasonable members, who take a stance and dig in and are very ideological, often need to be placated, whereas the team players who are relied upon to be reasonable don't always get due recognition for what they do. As a result, I frequently underestimate myself and what I'm capable of. However, throw me into a situation where I'm forced to produce out of my comfort zone and I can do it. You just have to believe you can rise to the occasion.

The inner voice is usually a lot harder to deal with than the put-downs of others. But for me it's like this: I show up for work, I do the best I that I can, and if I don't succeed at what I'm trying to accomplish, I can learn from that. We sometimes learn a lot more from our failures than we do from consistent success; therefore it really boils down to making the attempt. Just as you can't win the lottery if you don't buy a ticket, you can't accomplish your goals if you don't try. And if somebody says you can't achieve something for whatever reason, who says you can't? You never know what you're capable of until you try.

# 4

## Be Brave. Be Prepared. And When You're Not, Fake It.

The importance of formal education and those tough lessons life deals us can't be overstated. Since our mother had to drop out of school to help raise her four siblings after their father died, she was determined that all seven of her children would graduate college. However, she also never gave up on *herself*, embracing a new culture by boldly jumping into the unfamiliar American world of Avon, Little League, and the PTA, while returning to school and emerging with a college degree at age forty-five during an era when older students were virtually nonexistent.

Our father, who supported her efforts, was a hard taskmaster in terms of our own education, yet we always managed to deliver. Indeed, Loretta was the first Head Start student to ever make it to the halls of Congress, with Linda following close behind. During our first days on Capitol Hill we each benefited from our great-aunt Betty's advice: closely observe those around you, mimic them, and never let on that you didn't know how to do everything all along.

## LORETTA

Our mother initially lived in Sonora, a Mexican state that shares a border with Arizona to the north. After her father died she had to take care of her four siblings because she was the oldest girl. In Mexico, a daughter was automatically expected to help around the home, while a son would work to support the family. So Mom cooked, cleaned, and kept everything together while her own mother was out working, and that meant she never had much of a childhood.

For generations, the family had barely eked out an existence, but our grandmother had a sister, our great-aunt Betty, who lived in Los Angeles, and so the family joined her there when our mom was nine or ten. They lived above a Chinese restaurant in downtown L.A. and did quite nicely on the job front until somebody reported them for being in the country without the required legal documents. That led to them being sent back to Mexico, not back to Sonora, but to Mexicali, the northernmost city in Baja California, Mexico, which, as the name suggests, shares a border with California. And although they were in a place where they knew no one, on the day of their arrival, our grandmother went out and got a job sewing mattress covers for a dollar apiece.

## LINDA

After Mom's older brother went to L.A. and joined the U.S. Army, he became an American citizen and was then able to petition for the immigration of his mother and siblings. Mom was eighteen when they arrived in America, but instead of having an easier time she now had to deal with her strict older brother, who didn't want her to go out, have fun, and possibly disgrace the family.

Protecting a woman's honor is paramount within the Latino culture, and I remember Mom telling me about the time her brother forbade her and their younger sister Lydia from attending a neighborhood party where there'd be dancing. After secretly putting on their party dresses, they climbed under the bedcovers, pretended to fall asleep, and waited for him to doze off before sneaking away. He, however, quickly caught on and locked them out, so when they returned around midnight they had to sleep on the porch. That's the kind of rigidity Mom was used to when growing up.

## LORETTA

Dad grew up in Nogales, a city on the northern border of Sonora, the youngest of four siblings in a mountaintop home that had running water and an outhouse. The family had a good name, but, as is often the case in that part of the world, it no longer had the associated money. This may have been partly due to the trouble encountered by Dad's father, a judge without a law degree, who was always siding with the people instead of the government that had appointed him. Dad attended school through the seventh or eighth grade, and then he, like everyone else there during the Depression, was expected to make a living. So, that's what he did, running a bicycle store, working as a cobbler, playing pool, and basically doing whatever he could to make money.

He was a smart, good-looking, going-nowhere-fast kind of guy, and eventually he decided to strike out on his own and try his luck in the United States. So, in 1950, at age twenty-five, he came here and landed a job in a cannery. Years later he told me about those days, about how he got his first paycheck, didn't know how to cash it, and ended up having it cashed at the local saloon. By the next day it was all gone. "I was so wet behind the ears," he said. "What did I know?" But then, that's been the story for so many immigrants—Where do you find a place to stay? How do you set up a bank account? Dad faced these struggles and learned from on-the-job training. It was hit-and-miss, as it is for all immigrants. Nobody takes you by the hand and says, "Let me show you how."

## LINDA

Mom was doing bookkeeping at a big rubber-plastics factory in L.A. when she and Dad met. There were efforts to unionize the line workers, and one of the union representatives approached Mom and asked her to help persuade them to hold an election on this issue. She agreed, and among the people she talked to was our father. They began dating when she was nineteen—he was twelve years older than she was—married in 1957, and soon after started a family.

Right from the start, Mom was the homemaker and Dad was the breadwinner. They shared an apartment with her mother in the city of Compton, staying there until they could scrape together the down payment and finances for an $18,000 house in El Monte, where they again lived with Grandma, as well as with their first four children and Mom's younger brother, Victor. Unfortunately, it wasn't long before Uncle Victor got into trouble. He was using drugs and involved with gangs, and when someone drove by one day and shot through the front windows of the El Monte house, our father decided enough was enough. He didn't want his kids growing up around this, so he and Mom looked around and found a house in Anaheim that was in foreclosure.

At that time, Anaheim was largely orange groves. Disneyland had opened a couple of years earlier and it still wasn't all that well known, so aside from a Rockwell facility for engineers and scientists, as well as the trains passing through to collect the citrus, there wasn't a lot going on. That's why, when the rest of the family heard about the move to Orange County, they thought my father was crazy. Still, he purchased the house and that's where the three youngest siblings—me included—were born.

We were, quite literally, the first Mexican family in the neighborhood. And as soon as the neighbors on either side learned that Mexicans were moving in, they both put their homes up for sale. It didn't matter that Anaheim had been founded by German immigrants back in the 1850s. We were the wrong type of immigrants. The families who lived there must have thought, "Okay, there goes the neighborhood," and so they packed up and moved a few blocks away. Nevertheless, we still went to school with their children, and all of us became very close friends, even taking vacations together. Years later the mother of one family told our mom that she now regretted what they had done. "I'm so sorry," she apologized. "We knew nothing about you."

## LORETTA

But being Mexican wasn't the only way our family was different. The aerospace industry was in Anaheim, and our dad was pretty much the only blue-collar worker in the very middle-class neighborhood where we lived. Most of our friends' fathers were engineers.

## LINDA

Neither of our parents spoke much English when they arrived in this country, and so while Dad took classes to learn a skilled trade at L.A. Technical College, he also took English classes. There he met immigrants from other countries, and they were all in the same boat, trying to learn a new language. Sometimes, after class, they'd visit L.A.'s different ethnic neighborhoods to eat the food of one of their group—one day they'd eat Italian food, the next Greek, and so on—and this really helped broaden their experience, our father's included.

By the time he and Mom were living in Anaheim, they were both able to converse in English, although at home we spoke Spanish. Dad did manual labor until he acquired the skills to become an industrial mechanic and a machinist; Mom was raising a growing family and doing jobs in her spare time to bring in extra money. She cleaned houses, sold Stanley products and Avon cosmetics, and was forever trying to find ways to make ends meet. The interruption of her schooling, when she stayed home to take care of her siblings, meant she never realized her dreams of becoming a nurse. However, she wanted her children to have the opportunity to pursue their dreams, and so our education was very important to her, as it was to our father. They saw it as the key to success in this country, the way to get yourself off the factory floor and into the windowed offices. That's why they were adamant about us doing well at school.

In fact, my mother could be absolutely fierce about making sure we got the best education possible. I remember when I went to sign up for classes my freshman year of high school. We had moved into a new school district, and the counselors didn't have my records, because they hadn't yet been transferred. My mother and I sat in one counselor's office while she wrote out my class schedule and explained what courses were required. When my mother saw that I had been signed up for general education classes and remedial language arts (English), she was shocked. She told the counselor that I had been in honors and advanced classes in junior high, and that she wanted to see me continue in the college prep track. The counselor tried explaining that the honors classes were already full, and that they simply didn't have the desk space for another student. "Well then," my mother replied, "Linda will sit on the floor if she has to so that she can take those classes." By this point, the counselor understood that my mom was not going to take no for an answer. Needless to say, they ended up "finding" the space to fit me in.

## LORETTA

And Dad had definite ideas about what was important for us to know. When he had to sign off on the classes

I would take, he knew exactly which ones they should be—"You're going to take algebra, you're going to take physics, you're going to take chemistry, you're going to take biology." He had a whole list. And since he made the decisions, there was no way I was going to be studying something like underwater basket weaving. By the time it got to Linda, however, he wasn't so strict with the sign-off program, so she had more flexibility to pick her own subjects.

In my case, Mom had no role in this. Dad was the one who decided on the classes, he was the one who reviewed the report cards, and he was the one who meted out the discipline that pertained to them. After all, we were expected to bring home only A's. If one of us had a bad time or something was going on we could slip and get a B—although *I* was never allowed to get a B! I always got straight A's, and Dad didn't even need to open the report card to know that. At one time I thought about getting a B just to see if he'd notice, but of course I couldn't do it. I had the responsibility of setting the path for the other kids, and deviating just wasn't in my vocabulary.

There was no doubt in Dad's mind that his kids were going to get A's. He was *incredibly* strict. You had to take all the right classes, you had to get straight A's, and that was that. Still, we had one brother who didn't—not because he was dumb, he was actually probably one of the smartest of our whole bunch, but sometimes smart people are just way *too* smart for the rest of the world. They don't think the way the rest of the class does, and that was my brother Frank, who was the third kid among seven in our family. He would bring home B's and C's, and Dad would whip him. In Dad's book, if you got a C it was because you were lazy, and there was no place for laziness in our family.

The threat was always there, and it didn't matter how old you were: "You don't do well at school and I'm sending you to Mexico. I'm going to make you work on the farm." We actually thought he *owned* a farm somewhere, or knew somebody who did, and that we'd be put to work in a cornfield. For me that was the scariest thing—working like a burro all day long! It was a good enough reason to obey orders and never get distracted. And that's how I am today—I rarely get distracted by other influences or forces around me, and I think that's a result of how I coped with the family dynamic when growing up.

As my brother Henry says, "You'd just sit down and read your encyclopedia," and it's true. Dad bought me this great set of encyclopedias—actually, he bought them for the family, but they were *mine*—and it was just so amazing to read those books. I'd sit myself down in a corner and block out all the noises going on in our three-bedroom home that accomodated nine people. And to a large extent I'm still like that—I work quite a bit, but I also like to read my books, listen to my music, and generally do my own thing.

# LINDA

The fact that our father wanted his daughters to get an education was really kind of astonishing for that time period. But then, since both he and Mom had already moved to a new country in search of a better life, it's logical—if not traditional—that they'd want this for all their children. You have to remember, people who leave their families behind, as Dad did, and emigrate to the United States are usually risk takers and highly motivated. They're moving away from their loved ones, their culture, and everything they know to live in a country where they have no idea what they're going to encounter, and as such they're trailblazers. This is partially why I get upset when I hear people say immigrants are lazy. Few would be prepared to do what they do.

Whereas Dad only had two elderly great-aunts living here when he moved, Mom was surrounded by a number of close relatives who could help her, yet what she did was still extraordinary. And having lived very hard lives before they met, the number one goal in both our parents' minds was for their kids to have something better. They knew—and I appreciate this more and more as I grow older—that it would require plenty of sacrifice on their part, but God bless them, they were undeterred. Back then, it was normal for Latinos to believe that supporting the family was the most important thing, and that either the boys should quit school as young as possible to earn money, or that, in order for them to get a college education, the girls would have to stay home and help run the household. After all, they'd only be getting married and having kids anyway.

Within that context, it was revolutionary for our parents to not only ensure that their boys didn't drop out of school, but to also want their girls to attend college. It wasn't the same for our cousins. One of Mom's brothers actually told our parents, "You guys are stupid. Make your sons get jobs to help support the family. You don't need education. All you need is a good job."

If, initially, our father was more pro education for his sons than for his daughters, there was a turning point. The union-organizing campaign that brought Mom and him together failed, so he wasn't represented by a union at work and he never had health care benefits. That was difficult with seven kids. Our parents had to pay cash for all our doctors' and dentists' visits, sometimes up front and sometimes on a payment plan, including when my younger brother and I both broke our arms. Well, when I was in second grade, Dad got injured on the job and he was unable to work for about two weeks. "What would happen to us if something happened to you?" Mom asked him. "I would be left, trying to provide for seven children. That's why I'm going back to school, so that if anything ever does happen to you I can support the family."

Soon after, in addition to raising seven children with the elder siblings' help, she began attending night classes at a local community college. And while our father wasn't too happy about this, he also saw the sense in what Mom was doing. Each class would run from about 7:00 to 10:00 p.m., so beforehand she would make dinner, leave it warming in the oven, and tell me, "Linda, when your dad gets home, all you have to do is ask him if he wants to eat and serve him dinner." Then she'd go.

My job as the youngest daughter, when Dad arrived home exhausted and sat on the porch, was to unlace his boots, take them off his feet, and tell him I'd serve dinner whenever he was hungry. Well, there were a few times when he replied, "I'm not hungry just yet. Let me rest. I'll be hungry in a while." An hour later I'd ask, "Dad, should I serve you now?" and he'd answer, "Uh, not yet. I'll let you know when I'm ready to eat."

He would keep doing this until Mom arrived home sometime after ten o'clock, ensuring that *she* served him dinner. The point he was trying to make: even though she was going to school, she was still bound by her responsibilities at home. That meant she had to deal with seven kids during the day, prepare Dad's dinner at night, go to college for three hours, and then serve him his meal and clean the dishes before going to bed. It was quite a schedule.

## LORETTA

Absolutely. There were many times when Mom also asked me to serve Dad his dinner, and this came with the instruction to warm his tortillas at just the right time. You see, in a Mexican household it's not enough to warm the tortillas and put them on the table—no, no, no, you must warm them as the man needs them. Just as he's finishing the ones that are in front of him, you're taking care of the next batch so that they're warm to the fingertips precisely when he wants them. Well, that's what I made sure to do, but when I served Dad his food he'd invariably ask, "Where's your mother?"

I'd tell him, "She went to night school," and he'd say, "Oh, she's just out on the street. She's not even cooking for me!"

"Dad, she cooked the meal—"

"She's not here to serve it!"

"But Dad, *I'm* here to serve it—"

"That's not good enough! Your mother's supposed to be at home, taking care of me."

He would have big fights with her, often right before she went to class, and all because he wanted her at home. However, Mom knew that she really needed an education, and so she continued to go even though Dad threw up all these hurdles.

## LINDA

Don't forget, to attend college she'd first had to pass her GED tests, and that had taken her a while because she had a family to take care of and help support. Now night classes were added to the mix, and as she became better educated and more exposed to American culture during the early to mid-seventies, she started to question some of the very strict rules that the Latino culture applied to men and women.

This didn't mean Mom became a feminist. She just began to see how, in this country, wives weren't treated quite so much as maids. Yes, that kind of thing still went on, but at least women could also have real jobs outside the home, and I remember her telling me when I was young, "Try to marry an American man, because he'll help his wife with the dishes and even take her out to eat once a week." That, of course, was a commentary on her own marriage. Dad didn't do anything domestic, and whereas Mom became a little more open to U.S. culture, he wanted things to remain as they'd always been back in Mexico. And why wouldn't he? He had it good.

Interestingly, while there was friction between Mom and me about how the boys in our family were treated differently from the girls, on one level she could understand my point because she'd experienced that in her marriage. She understood that women were—for lack of a better word—oppressed within the Latino culture, but by the same token she still couldn't help treating the boys differently most of the time. Some women, once they'd taken note of that, might have been more apt to understand their daughters and try to make things a little more equitable. However, the gender roles within our family were so clearly defined that, even though Mom didn't like how she was expected to conform, she also didn't try to combat that for the rest of us.

Still, during the period when she was about to graduate college, she'd tell the girls, "Get an education, travel, and see the world before you get married. Don't marry at a young age like I did and get tied down with a family." No longer young enough to become a nurse, Mom studied to become a teacher, inspired by a part-time job that she'd had working as a teacher's assistant, where she'd helped a lot of immigrant kids who were pretty much being ignored and left behind in many of the classrooms. She'd become something of an advocate and an activist for them, and so she then decided to make teaching her career. At age forty-five, after about six years of studying, she graduated from Cal State Fullerton. To my mind, just raising seven kids should earn someone the Congressional Medal of Honor. But doing that and going to college? Amazing.

This was at a time when the concept of older returning students still wasn't all that well known. College was for young kids right out of high school, and I remember her telling me about how she'd declined an invitation to join some of them for coffee and a study group in preparation for an exam. She felt embarrassed because she was so much older than all of them. However, when she graduated, we all attended the ceremony and cheered really loudly, yelling in unison, "Way to go, Mom!" I'm sure Dad was very proud of her, too. By then, he was earning more money, but he still welcomed the extra income that would result from her teaching. And since the hours she'd work would coincide with those of our school schedules, he was comfortable in the knowledge that she'd be home with the family each afternoon.

## LORETTA

Our father eventually became the equivalent of an industrial engineer. He would retool rubber-plastics factories, take care of production lines, deal with mechanical problems, even do welding. He was incredibly gifted, and to a large extent he was also self-taught—a case of doing the best he could under the circumstances. His situation reminds me of a Vietnamese janitor I met while he was throwing out the trash when I was an investment banker. By talking to him I learned that back in Vietnam he'd been a university professor teaching Chinese philosophy! Some people have to do whatever comes their way when they move to a new country. That's the plight of the immigrant.

## LINDA

Although Mom's studying did create some friction between her and our dad, in the end it helped both of them grow as people. They desperately wanted to understand American culture and make sure we were a part of it like everybody else. They thought that would be an advantage down the line. And while there was friction with mostly the older children over issues such as Loretta's being on the flag team yet not being allowed to go to the football games, our parents did learn to adapt over time, and one of the things that helped them become involved—especially in our extracurricular school activities—was Loretta's being a Head Start student.

Launched in the summer of 1965 as part of President Lyndon Johnson's "War on Poverty"—and still in operation today—the Head Start program was designed to provide preschool children from low-income familes with comprehensive education, health, and nutritional care. At the same time it sought to involve parents in their kids' education and get them acquainted with a school system that can be extremely difficult for immigrants to understand and navigate. Loretta was one of the first kids in that pilot program, and not only did it benefit her, but it also taught Mom a lot while introducing her to other parents and served to make her more comfortable with the whole system.

## LORETTA

As much as this may surprise anyone who now knows me, I was a very shy child, and Head Start helped me take the first steps toward dealing with that. Before, I didn't speak English or Spanish to anybody, and my grandmother kept taking me to the doctor and insisting

I was deaf and mute. The doctor would take a look at me and tell her, "She's just not ready to talk to you." The only person I really spoke to was my older brother Henry, but we had our own language. I would communicate with him and he'd then interpret for Mom: she wants this or she wants that. For all intents and purposes, I was indeed mute. And I was so shy that in almost every picture taken of me I was crying. I hated being photographed. I was a *mess,* and my mother knew it.

When she read in the newspaper about this new summer school program that would help underprivileged kids and minorities to compete at the same level as other kids, she said, "This program's for Loretta. She needs *help.*" So, she got me into Project Head Start. I remember her walking me over to Legore Elementary School, which was just three houses from where we lived in El Monte, on that first day and trying to leave me there. I started screaming and grabbing onto her legs, but she left anyway, and I was distraught. I cried and cried and cried, and the only thing that calmed me down was snack time. They handed out watermelon and sticks of celery with peanut butter, and all of a sudden this was better than home. My mom wasn't a snack kind of person, so after that I couldn't wait to go to school.

Head Start is now a year-round program but back then it lasted eight weeks, and during that time I not only learned colors, numbers, and how to write, but also how to talk, share, play, and interact with other kids. The shyness would last until Dad made me take speech class in seventh grade, but that preschool experience was invaluable, and it was very helpful to Mom as well.

## LINDA

When many immigrants come here—and this applied to our parents—they're often shy, mistrustful, and unsure of what to expect within a totally unfamiliar setup. Then again, they also don't want to be perceived as stupid, so they're walking a fine line between "Okay, how can I find out about this?" and openly admitting "I don't know a thing," which could leave them wide open to exploitation. Mom and Dad found this tough to deal with, but it became easier with each child. And today, whenever I get stuck on a problem or I'm afraid to try something, I think about how hard it must have been for my parents to make their way after leaving behind everything they knew, and for Mom to show up on a community college campus and navigate that system all on her own. I try to reduce my anxiety and fear by telling myself, "Hey, you can't be defeated before you even start."

Early in 2007, after four years in Congress, I had the opportunity to become chairman of a judiciary subcommittee, but I was a little hesitant. I'd never been in charge of a subcommittee before, setting the agenda and running the mechanics, and so, given my age, inexperience, and unfamiliarity with the issues, there was definitely a moment of self-doubt regarding whether or not I was up to the challenge. When I discussed this with a supporter and mentor of mine, Mike Tuchin, he really encouraged me to take the chairmanship. I thought about my parents, whose attitude has always been that opportunities arise very rarely, and that sometimes you have to go beyond what you think you're capable of, even masking your lack of confidence by pretending, if necessary, that you know what you're doing, and acting as if you've been doing this your whole life. If you put in the work, things will be okay.

Again, I thought about the adversity my parents had faced, about the nerve it had taken for Mom to attend school in a foreign country and emerge with a college degree, and consequently I ended up taking the chairmanship of the subcommittee. Since this dealt with bankruptcy law and mundane administrative law, it was actually like the dark-haired stepchild compared to other subcommittees that handled sexier issues pertaining to constitutional or criminal law. Accordingly I expected a sleepy little subcommittee that would be good for me to cut my teeth on as a chairwoman. After all, without huge, controversial topics it would be largely overlooked, and as it turned out I actually had to beg some senior members to help me by being on that subcommittee as well. Nobody wanted to serve on it.

Then, out of nowhere, bam! One of the biggest issues that Congress had to deal with all year fell into my lap: the scandal over the firings of the the U.S. attorneys by Attorney General Alberto Gonzales. My subcommittee had jurisdiction over this issue, and suddenly everybody wanted to serve on it, even though there were no spaces because we had already filled them. There I was, still learning my job along with the parliamentary rules, and the second hearing I ever chaired involved the testimony of some of the fired attorneys. The bright lights of the media were all focused on what was going on, and not only did I wield the gavel, but I also had to do so in a way that convinced people I was completely comfortable and that I knew what I was doing.

For me, this was an important lesson in believing that, when called upon to stretch yourself and tackle a challenge that you're not sure you can handle, you just have to go for it and pretend it's nothing new. When it came to the hearing, I wanted it to be fair, and I wanted to appear that I was in control. I didn't want to be a tyrant with the gavel, but I did want people to know that I meant business and that we were there to discuss the issues.

In a hearing, each member is usually given five minutes to make an opening statement and then five minutes for questioning. However, if someone uses up his or her time, other members can yield their own time to enable that member to finish questioning. That's what happened with me. As chairwoman, I'd asked my questions first and used up my time, so Mel Watt, a Democratic member from North Carolina, yielded me two minutes of his time and wanted to reserve the remaining three minutes for when it was his turn to ask questions. The ranking Republican member from Utah objected, arguing that a member must either use his or her minutes all at once, or yield them all at once, but not split them up. Well, I didn't know the answer to that, and meanwhile the two members were bickering back and forth, ignoring the rules and procedures, until finally I had to gavel to restore order.

"The chairwoman will take the question under advisement," I announced. "In the meantime, since my time has expired, the ranking member from Utah is recognized for five minutes to ask questions." I just made that up, but it worked. Everybody quieted down, the questioning continued, and meanwhile staff checked the procedural rules and then told us it was true—we *couldn't* split time. By then everything had calmed down anyway, but at least I'd been able to solve the problem without having to stop the entire proceedings. That's all part of pretending you know what you're doing when in reality you don't. It's not about lying. It's about taking a moment to collect yourself, and controlling emotions to solve problems rationally.

After all, if I'm speaking at a public event and get asked a question that I don't know the answer to, the worst thing I can do is make up an answer, because that will come back to haunt me. Instead, I'll say, "I'm not sure. It could be x, y, or z, but I'll need to get back to you on this." In everyday life, when people are asked questions that they don't know the answers to, you can always tell if they're making things up as they go along. It's painful to watch. So, acting like you know what you're doing requires sound judgment.

## LORETTA

One of the things I learned from our dad early on was that you have to be disciplined, and that you can't always opt for the easy way out. That applied when he signed off on the classes I would take at school. It was always about having a good foundation. "In order to have a good foundation, you must take chemistry." "In order to understand how the world works, you must take physics." "In order to understand what is going on, you must take history." For him, these building blocks would enable you to perform whatever job or opportunity you were given. And so the message was: don't try to go the easy route. Take care of the fundamentals.

Even in the House of Representatives, if you don't understand the basics of a bill, you won't be able to pass it. If you don't understand the rules of the committee or the rules of the House, your opponents will use those rules against you. So, there are some fundamental things you have to learn: how a bill is created, where the power lies, how people can obstruct what you're trying to do. In the beginning, I didn't sit down and read the rules of the committee to figure out how somebody could mess with me, and as a result I often didn't even *know* they were messing with me! However, after being messed with a couple of times I thought, "I'd better go back and read those rules. I'd better know *exactly* what's going on." It's like chess — you have to think ahead. You have to know the moves they can make against you and prepare yourself to counter them.

When I first entered the House and I was on the Military Committee, I had a large Vietnamese population that I represented in my Congressional district. Unlike other committees, the Military handles one big bill for the entire year, dealing with issues such as how many people we're going to have in the military, what we're going to pay them, what kind of health care we're going to provide, how many B2 bombers we're going to buy, and so on. Everything's put in the same bill, so I wanted to propose an amendment that would state that the Vietnamese people had fought valiantly alongside us in the Vietnam War. This entailed my making a hundred copies of the amendment and then explaining it to my colleagues before it went to a vote.

Consisting of just eight sentences, it was really straightforward and basically a no-brainer. Nobody ever challenges you on that sort of thing...or so I thought. At that point, I wasn't yet a full member of the House, and there were those who wanted to oust me from the Congress and prevent me from having any success whatsoever. Accordingly, when I proposed the amendment there were immediate groans from the other side. They didn't even want me to read it because it was a no-brainer and everyone wanted to move on. But, after I introduced it, Steve Buyer from Indiana took a point of order—which I didn't even understand at the time—and substituted my amendment with his *own* amendment. This thanked the South Vietnamese, the Australians, the Thais, the South Koreans, the New Zealanders, and the Filipinos, who had been involved in the conflict. So, there it was, a much larger bill that said the same thing as mine, but added all these other nationalities and had *his* name on it.

We debated this for two hours, going back and forth, and when we finally took a vote, I of course lost. Now we had the Buyer substitute amendment, and I was really mad, but what I'd done when I knew I was going to lose was get my staff to prepare another hundred copies of my own amendment, incorporating a change to just one of the sentences. Then, after the vote was in, I turned to Mr. Skelten, the ranking member, and said, "Mr. Skelten, I have another amendment at the desk."

He said, "What would that amendment be about, Miss Sánchez?"

I said, "That amendment would be about recognizing the Vietnamese people in the Vietnam War."

He said, "The amendment being passed out is

*different* from the one that was previously offered. Is that correct?"

I said, "Yes, Mr. Skelten, I've changed one of the sentences."

He said, "Thank you."

By now my staff had told me what I had to do to make sure Steve Buyer couldn't substitute. However, before I could say something he tried to raise a point of order. Thankfully, the chairman, Floyd Spence, cut him off. "Is there any discussion on the amendment? If not, I call for the question."

This was a Republican chairman, basically saying, "Pipe down and let this lady get her stuff done." It was very kind on his part. I put forward my amendment and they voted yes. But quite frankly, if it hadn't been for the chairman giving me another chance, I wouldn't have been able to get it done. It was all about the pettiness of certain members who were trying to get rid of me, as well as the fairness of Mr. Spence, who could just as easily have said, "We've gone through that, Miss Sánchez. You're not going to introduce that again."

The thing is, had I known the rules, I could have stopped Steve Buyer the first time around. I could have argued the point of order with him, but I didn't know how to do that, and I also didn't understand what he and others were capable of doing. You have to know the basics, you have to be prepared. Constantly. This happens every day. It happens on the House floor, and we always have a member who knows the rules of order. There are a number of them who, when they enter the House, spend hours and hours just sitting there, watching the debate, studying how people raise points of order, and they become experts. So, when you're down there, debating a bill, and you're aware that the other side is going to play with you, you must have somebody from your own side who can jump in and know how to stop that. Some members know the rules in and out very, very well, and that's vital. Because no matter what you're doing, you have to know the rules of the game.

# 5

## Don't Eat the Grapes

We believe it's essential to decide what truly matters and then act in accordance with these convictions, a principle we absorbed largely from observing our mother. When grapes were banned from our dining table in support of the United Farm Workers' boycott, she took us to meet César Chávez, and she remains an activist to this day. It's probably from her that we inherited our stubborn but effective *rebelde* (rebellious) streak.

If we believe in something–whether it relates to education, workers' rights, or ourselves–we do whatever we think is warranted. This includes Loretta visiting all 166 schools within her district,

Linda providing pro bono legal services to mistreated migrant workers, and asking for funds for our campaigns.

We're not afraid to make difficult decisions in order to maintain the integrity of our convictions. It was the Republican Party's rightward drift and resulting alienation of women and minorities, for instance, that prompted Loretta's 1992 switch to the Democratic Party. Walking the walk – something that is so important, even when it requires a major adjustment.

## LORETTA

César Chávez was the great Mexican American civil rights activist who co-founded the National Farm Workers Association. This would later evolve into the United Farm Workers (UFW), and in 1965, following the example of Filipino American farm workers who had protested in favor of higher wages, he and the UFW led a strike of California grape pickers. These people were often sprayed with pesticides, had no bathroom facilities out in the fields, and were being paid piecemeal by the box, so César helped organize them, calling upon Americans everywhere to show their support by boycotting table grapes in order to force the growers toward the bargaining table.

We'd go grocery shopping every Sunday when I was a kid, and I *loved* green table grapes. However, every time I tried to put some in the cart, Dad would stop me and Mom would say, "César told us to not eat them, so we're not going to." They, like many others within the community, believed it was our duty to stand by the workers, and although the strike lasted many years, it eventually resulted in the first major labor victory for U.S. farm workers.

Sometime later, when I was nineteen or twenty and already living by myself in Anaheim, Mom called early one morning and told me to take a shower and get dressed because she was going to drive me somewhere. "Where?" I asked. "It doesn't matter," she replied. "Just get ready and I'll be by to pick you up." She arrived at around 7:00 a.m., Linda was with her, and she wouldn't tell either of us where we were going. Instead, we drove all the way from Orange County to San Luis Obispo, a four-hour journey, and then walked into a luncheon where Mom said, "I want you to meet one of my friends." Her friend was César Chávez.

As a teacher, Mom belonged to the Association of Mexican American Educators, and she had been working on political issues like migrant children's rights in the classroom. She was the organization's treasurer at the state level, and since she collected the political money and decided who it should be given to, she knew all of the politicians and union leaders. Among them was César, and when she introduced him to us — the two future congresswomen — I was quite honestly astounded that such a legendary man would be dressed so modestly, wearing worker's clothes and a sweatsuit jacket. It was a humbling experience. And it also taught me about retaining your integrity when sticking to your principles.

Whereas Mom was a compassionate Democrat, Dad ended up running his own business and reading the libertarian *Orange County Register*, so he was very antitax and pro-Republican. Neither of them voted back then — they owned land in Mexico, and to do so they had to be Mexican citizens. Since dual citizenship with America wasn't allowed before 1994, they didn't become U.S. citizens until a couple of years after that. By then, like me, Dad had converted from Republican to Democrat.

The first time I registered to vote was in social studies class at high school when I turned eighteen. The teacher was a Democrat, but when I asked what I should register as, he said, "Well, unfortunately here in Orange County, if you want to vote in the primary and have a choice, you've got to be a Republican, because the Democrats don't have any choices. This is a Republican place." So, I registered as a Republican and I would vote like any other citizen; voting for someone I knew, had heard of, or who was quite simply a woman. I constantly crossed party lines. In fact, the first election campaign I worked on at that time was for a Democrat running for Congress—he was running against Bob Dornan! Not that I knew who Bob Dornan was. I just happened to go along to a meeting with friends who were politically active, and I heard this man speak and decided to help out.

The person I campaigned for was a really wonderful man named Dave Carter, who today is a U.S. federal judge in Orange County and has taken on the Mexican Mafia and many other high-profile cases. He lost in the primary, so he never went up against Dornan directly, but we walked door-to-door for him, and when I went to sign the "We're Going to Win with Dave Carter" banner for the end-of-campaign celebration, lo and behold, my sister Linda's name was on it! She was in high school at the time, and it turned out that she had also been working for his campaign.

I remained registered as a Republican and never really thought about it much. That was, until one night when I was flicking through the TV channels at home and just happened to catch Pat Buchanan making an inflammatory speech, calling for an end to immigrants coming to America. I was so angry that a high-profile Republican was allowed to spew that kind of hatred on national televison, the very next day I registered as a Democrat.

This didn't coincide with a change in my philosophy. It was really just a case of my becoming more informed. I'm a fiscally conservative Democrat, so I brought my businesswoman sensibilities with me, and since most of labor lines up with the Democrats there was no problem in my having been a five-year member of the United Food and Commercial Workers union when scooping ice cream at Sav-On.

I've changed my views on certain issues with the passing years just like anybody does. People often tend to get more conservative as they grow older, and maybe in some areas that's happened to me. In others, I've perhaps gone more liberal. I'm very capable of changing my mind on an issue if there's information that tells me, "What you thought, Loretta, just wasn't the case." I really don't have a problem with that. I made the switch from Republican to Democrat and never looked back because I knew what I was doing was right for me. And that's been the case whenever I've felt the need to stand up for my convictions.

When Linda was thirteen, she was involved with Bobby Sox Softball. In order for her team to play, it needed a female manager—the coach could be a man, but a woman had to be present at all times. Well, since I had just turned eighteen and the moms were all working, Linda phoned me at work to ask if I'd take the job. I said

I would, and while I quickly discovered that I'd been put in charge of a team comprised of a bunch of leftovers and the obligatory pair of all-stars from the year before — one of whom was Linda — we ended up surprising everybody by winning one of the three complete rounds and making it to the final. The team we faced, which included the league president's daughter, had been the hot favorite right from the get-go, and sure enough, they had won two of the three complete rounds. However, thanks to a rule agreed upon during a meeting of all the league's managers, there would only be a one-game play-off in order to win the title.

At the meeting, I had actually stated it would be fairer if we played a best-of-three-game series, since during the regular season we played three complete rounds. But the league president disagreed: "One game, and that's it. Whoever wins that game takes it all."

"But that doesn't seem very fair…"

"Yes, it's fine. One game will decide it."

So, that's what I told my girls: "You just have to win this *one game* and you'll be the champs!" Well, guess what happened. The game was scheduled to last seven innings, and by the fifth inning we were winning, at which point the president came over to me and said, "Oh, Loretta, I was wrong. If you win this game you'll still have to play again."

I looked at her in disbelief. "You don't change the

rules at this stage," I remarked, to which she said, "But these are the *national* rules. We were just wrong."

There was no way I was buying it. "I was the one who stood up and *said* you were wrong, but you still insisted we'd only play one game. So, that's what we're doing. We're only playing one game."

Unable to work her charm on me, Madam President now approached my girls and said, "You know if you win this game you'll still have to play again in a best-of-three series."

"Don't listen to this woman," I reassured them. "You carry on playing the game, and when you get this done, you'll be the winners."

That's precisely what happened. We ended up winning, and we celebrated our victory. Then, the following week, I received a call from a woman at Bobby Sox Softball's national headquarters, telling me, "There needs to be a best-of-three series."

Again, I refuted that idea, pointing out how there'd been plenty of opportunity beforehand to get things right, and how everyone had been in the room when I'd actually stated I didn't think the one-game rule was fair. "You people were even around before the game started," I reminded her. "You could have come to me then and told me it was going to be a three-game series, but you waited until we were in the fifth inning to tell me that my girls weren't going to be winners. That's because you'd assumed we were going to lose, and it's totally unacceptable. You do not change the rules in the middle of the game. It's the principle of the thing."

A few days after our victory, the girls' mothers began receiving calls about the time and place of the next game. But I had already collected the uniforms and the mothers had told their girls to forget it while also informing the league officials, "My girl's not playing another game. She is a champion."

Since the league didn't want to recognize this, we had our own team party and bought the girls their own trophies, and in the end it was officially decided that the two teams would be "cochampions." The Bobby Sox people couldn't believe that I would refuse to give in to them, but people who know me know I can be stubborn when I think I'm right.

It's a daily struggle to do what you think you should be doing, and some things that appear really easy to do often turn out to be extremely ambitious. I mean, who would deny a group of girls a sports trophy? And while I may be determined to stand by my convictions, I also have to contend with other people's total lack of principle. I've had people tell me we have a deal on something, and then two minutes later they've walked up to the microphone in the Congress and revealed that they're doing the complete opposite. I've just stood there and thought, "Wow, I'm not going to trust *you* again." They've been that blatant.

We have a saying in the Congress: "I'm with you as long as I can be." People change their minds. And while some are obviously worse than others, I suppose that applies to all of us at one time or another. After all, some political votes are held just to make people look bad—they don't have any relevance or impact, but they're done to catch each other in a game of "gotcha." For example, the Republicans put up a resolution that states that not only are the troops doing a great job in the war, which is absolutely true, but that President Bush is also a great war leader…If you vote for it, people might say, "Why are you against the president when in the resolution you agreed he's a great war leader?" And if you don't vote for it, you could be in trouble for not supporting the troops anymore.

I tell you, those votes are utter stupidity no matter which way you lean, whereas one that gives the commander-in-chief the right to go to war has dire consequences—people dying—and cannot be taken lightly. That's why many who knew better and still opted to send our young men into Iraq subsequently wished they could take their vote back. Without a doubt, it was one of the most difficult issues I've personally ever had to vote on. There was tremendous pressure to go with the flow, but the bottom line for me: stick to my beliefs and don't give in to the bullies.

In 1998, President Clinton made me a cochair of the Democratic National Committee, and that saw me through the whole period when we were working on getting Al Gore into the White House. The year of the election, 2000, our national convention was scheduled to take place in Los Angeles, and as usual this would involve lots of free parties attended by all of the big donors. So, since I was also heading up a nonpartisan political action committee, Hispanic Unity USA, that was helping to register new Latino voters in time for the presidential election, I told my husband I was thinking of throwing a fund-raiser when the Democratic Convention–goers were in L.A.

"That's a great idea," he said. "The only thing is, the other parties will be free and yours won't."

Not at $5,000 per person, that's for sure. "Then what venue might serve as the biggest attraction?" I asked.

"Well" came the reply, "the best place, the really *in* place, the place where all the stars like to hang out is the Playboy Mansion. It's back in vogue."

I thought, "Okay, sounds good to me." So, I called Hugh Hefner and I asked him if it would be okay to throw the fund-raiser at his home.

"Loretta, I'll do whatever you want," Hef replied, "but are you sure you want to do that?"

"Why?" I asked.

"Well, you know, some people get weird when they hear the *Playboy* name."

"But Al Gore's taken your money," I countered, "and you've given hundreds of thousands of dollars to the Democratic Party. So, what's wrong with us throwing a fund-raiser at your place? You've been a contributor for many, many years."

"Okay," he said, "no problem."

After setting August 15 as the date, we put out the word, and the event was even listed on the official calendar that the Democratic National Committee (DNC) had on its website, detailing all of the things that would be going on during Convention week. Well, within no time at all, it became the one party that *everyone* wanted to attend. It took on a life of its own—people wanted to get onto the Convention floor and into the Playboy Mansion. And believe it or not, many of them were women. A total of 650 donors ended up on the guest list, yet at the end of May I received a phone call from one of Al Gore's campaign people telling me the event was a nonstarter because *Playboy's* image didn't tie in with Al's support for family values. Never mind that he'd already collected $1,500 in campaign money from Hef and his daughter, Christie.

I said, "Okay, well, you need to get me another house that'll be just as good. You know all the stars. Get me Barbra Streisand's house or somewhere else that'll work and we won't have a problem."

Well, *we* didn't have a problem, but apparently *I* did,

with the campaign operative's implying that if I didn't cancel the party at Hef's, I'd be a pariah in Washington. Obviously, he didn't know me very well. I was going to have the party, and that was that.

I'd given him an out—either he and his colleagues would find me a good place to host the party or it would take place at the mansion because I'd already sold all the tickets. I wasn't panicking. Then Henry Cisneros, the former Secretary of Housing and Urban Development, contacted me, saying Gore had asked him to reiterate that I wasn't to stage the fund-raiser. However, when I explained I was organizing it for a nonpartisan committee that was trying to register Hispanic voters, Henry said he thought it was a great idea.

"Then can I put your name down on the invitations as one of the hosts?" I asked.

"Sure," said Henry, "not a problem."

Later I was informed that Gore's people had also called another Latino, Bill Richardson, America's ambassador to the United Nations before being appointed Secretary of Energy. Bill pointed out that they were dealing with the woman who had beaten Bob Dornan, hardly someone afraid of a fight. And since I felt I was doing the right thing, he advised them to drop the whole issue.

That's what we thought they would do. With no other venue, they would just forget about it. They couldn't possibly make a big deal out of it...Oh man, they made a big deal. And they started doing so through the newspapers. They didn't even call me. They just told reporters they couldn't believe I was doing this, that they'd take away my position as cochair of the Democratic National Committee, and that they'd also pull the plug on my reelection campaign.

My reaction? Since nobody would take my calls, I just answered them back in the newspapers: Al Gore had taken money from Hugh Hefner, and if he didn't want to go to his house, that was okay, I wasn't asking him to. However, other people wanted to go there and help us raise money, so why not? What Hef does is legal. It's called First Amendment rights.

I couldn't believe Gore's people would leave him so wide open to that kind of response. But they did. Don't forget, he was going to be the next president and I was just some nothing, second-term congresswoman who didn't know what she was getting herself into. They'd destroy me in the papers. They honestly didn't figure that I'd stand up and say, "Hello? Does the public know, Al, that you take money from this guy but won't go to his home?" It was really dumb. I'd never seen so many people sweating bullets, but I kept telling them, "Hey, relax, it's not a big deal. They'll go away. We're in the right here. First Amendment rights are what Democrats stand for."

That's what sustained me. Every time Gore's people

tried to bully me, I pushed back, and although many people were initially questioning why a Latina would want to organize a party at the Playboy Mansion, they eventually realized this was a bipartisan political event with no Playmates in attendance. None had been around for other fund-raisers held there, benefiting everything from cancer research and arms control to women's causes, and we didn't need Bunnies to help us get out the Hispanic vote.

What, in my opinion, made Al Gore's people really mad was that we were raising a lot of money and it wasn't for *them*. It wasn't for the DNC, it wasn't for Democrats, it was for Latinos who hadn't yet registered, and despite Bill Richardson's pushing back and telling them to leave it alone, they couldn't leave it alone. I sat there thinking, "If you're aiming your ammunition at me instead of at your opponent, there's no way you're going to win this election."

The newspapers and television just kept running with the story, and two days before the Convention it was Sánchez versus Gore—who's going to win? A great big scandal had been created out of what should have been just a boring political get-together, but in the end most people understood what was going on and they sided with me—"Leave Sánchez alone. Why are you ganging up on this lady? Why did you take money from Hef if you don't think his image is 'right' for the Democrats?'"

The average person respected the fact that I was standing up to the vice president, but by then the dispute had become the major Convention issue and I didn't want it to shift the focus away from the Democratic platform, so I switched the party from the Playboy Mansion to the House of Blues on the Universal Studio lot and made it clear this wasn't about me. Still, that didn't prevent the Gore camp from publicly asserting that it was, and that I wanted all the attention for myself. My response was to go on television and announce that, despite my position as cochairman of the Convention, I wouldn't be speaking from the podium.

That created another scandal. And when I walked onto the floor I disrupted the Convention, with all these delegates standing in line to greet me, give me a hug, and shake my hand. These were the delegates who remembered that, when nobody wanted to go to Idaho and nobody wanted to go to Alabama and nobody wanted to go to Kansas or Missouri or Wyoming to give speeches, raise money, and provide help, that's what I had done. For two years I had crisscrossed the United States, visiting places that no one else did, and now on the floor of the Convention those delegates showed their appreciation. It was quite a moment, and it was about the principle. The delegates on the floor had saved me, and when the fund-raiser took place it was a great success.

You see, what people often don't understand about me is that, whereas most politicians have spent the better part of their lives to get where they are, I had a life before I entered politics and if I left the Congress tomorrow I'd find a hundred other things that I want to do. That means I'm not afraid of losing my position, and so I don't think like the majority of politicians who are always calculating how the right or wrong moves might impact their careers.

## LINDA

Our mom definitely taught us that there are times when we must stand up for our convictions and not back down. I remember when she was working as a teacher's assistant, she came home and told us about a student in her class who needed to use the rest room but was refused permission by the teacher because she should have gone there during recess. The child had ended up wetting her pants, and Mom was so appalled that she told us if we were ever in the same situation, we should get up and walk out anyway. In other words, defy authority if necessary, and be proactive rather than passive.

Mom ingrained that in us, and while Dad wasn't as vocal on the subject, there certainly were plenty of times when we saw him stand up for himself. One incident in particular was legendary within our neighborhood, dating back to our first house in Anaheim, located on Center Street. My brother Mike and I were both very young, and while we were asleep one afternoon some local yahoo was riding his motorcycle up and down the street, revving the engine and making a lot of noise. Dad went out there and told him to stop, and when the guy ignored him my father physically removed him from the motorcycle and made sure he got the message. That pest had been terrorizing the neighborhood for quite some time, and so all of the neighbors were happy.

Dad was an industrial mechanic, building and maintaining huge machines, and for many years he was known as the best at what he did. When he worked at the rubber-plastics factory he helped develop a system that streamlined the fabrication of a particular product. As an immigrant, Dad didn't know about patent law, or that he could have made a lot of money if he'd gotten a patent. Instead, he asked for a percentage of the profit and his boss refused. So, my father quit and started his own business, and that was kind of a turning point for him. Later in life he'd tell us, "When you work for somebody else you're making money for them. When you work for yourself, everything you earn is your own."

Dad gave employment opportunities to a lot of people who couldn't get hired—some of them ex-convicts—and he really believed in giving everyone a chance. I remember returning from trips to visit relatives in Mexico, and, as we crossed the border into San Diego, seeing long lines of people waiting to go through customs, along with vendors trying to sell Mexican souvenirs: piggy banks, blankets, you name it. Well, when Dad saw something he wanted, he'd call them over by yelling out, "Maestro." One time I asked him, "Why are you calling them 'Maestro'?" To me they were just peddlers, but he looked at me and he said, "They are masters at what they do, they are masters in their trade, and they deserve a level of respect."

His point was that every job, no matter how big or how small, is an important job. Whether you clean the streets and pick up the garbage or sit in a congressional office and pass legislation—everybody has value. That's why he and Mom treated everybody with respect, regardless of whether they were bosses or workers, and they always stuck up for people whom others judged, mocked, mistreated, or took advantage of. From a young age, I did the same, although I have to admit that, while this was partly due to our parents' example, it was also influenced by my dislike of how the boys and girls were treated differently in our family. I wanted more equality.

Being light-haired and light-skinned, none of us experienced much of the overt, ugly discrimination that was meted out to my darker-complexioned Hispanic schoolmates, such as a brother and sister named Mario and Claudia. Kids always made fun of them, yet the teacher would tell Claudia, "I'm sure that, if you tried harder, you could do as well as Linda." I thought that was really unfair. We all have different abilities in different areas, yet Claudia was told that she wasn't making the effort to succeed.

Our parents were very proud and never wanted government assistance of any kind. But when Dad was injured at work and didn't have an income for a couple of weeks, we qualified for free school lunches while he convalesced at home. The first day I was in that program, my teacher called out, "Okay, all of you free-lunch kids line up here and then go down to the office to get your meal." That was pretty much an announcement to the rest of the class: hey, these kids are different. Still, we collected our free lunch—which, by the way, tasted horrible—and when I returned to sit at the same table as my friends I was told, "You can't sit here. Go sit with the free-lunch kids." So, that's what I did, joining Claudia and Mario at another table, and we subsequently became friends. According to the pecking order, I now could eat lunch only with them, and that showed me not only how kids could be cruel, but how adults could unwittingly contribute to that.

Having been through this experience, I continued to talk and play with Claudia and Mario even after I resumed bringing my own lunch to school and was therefore allowed to sit at the regular table. And I always stuck up for them when they were teased by other kids. In fact, I virtually became a champion for the underdog.

In fourth grade, there was a Mexican girl who was really, really shy. She didn't have any friends, but I interacted with her quite a bit. Later on, when I attended a junior high that was extremely rough and had lots of gangs, she became the leader of this girl gang. They were the toughest chicks around, but when one of their members had a beef with me and wanted to beat me up after school one day, she intervened and said, "You leave her alone." Just one word from her and everyone listened. Nobody hassled me again after that. It's not like I had talked with her in fourth grade because someday she'd be able to do me a big favor. It was just natural that, if anybody was made to feel like an outsider, I'd make the effort to get to know them.

Our parents taught us to defend those who can't defend themselves, and that's very much a part of my work today. I see myself as somebody who advocates for people who don't have the wherewithal to do it for themselves, either because they're poor and don't have the resources, are unsophisticated about government, or just don't understand the legislative process. My job is to be a passionate advocate of those who are forgotten, those who are neglected, those who are ignored, those whom others don't consider to have much value, maybe because they're "just" gardeners or waitresses. These are people who, while trying to earn a living and keep their families together, are contributing to our economy, our communities, and our country. Yet others are attacking them. That's a large part of why I became a Democrat.

Sometimes I've encountered Republicans who seem to believe that people are poor because they choose to be poor, and that this wouldn't be the case if they just worked harder. Well, that isn't true. A lot of people start life with advantages that they don't even consider to be advantages, and I always point this out when I get into fights with my brother Ignacio, who's a Republican and fond of saying things like, "I pulled myself up by the bootstraps, and I'm successful because I worked hard."

I'll say, "Yes, and when you were in college and you were short of money, who did you call? You called Mom, and Mom sent you money. You also had loan programs that you could access. So, you didn't do it all on your own. In fact, you started out with advantages that many kids today don't have: a two-parent household, and a mom and dad who were involved in your schooling. A lot of kids don't have parents who pushed them hard to succeed or were there to help them when they fell a little bit short."

I believe there are two kinds of people in this life. There are those who succeed and attribute all the success to themselves—"I've got mine, you guys have to get yours." And then there are those who succeed and not only credit the teachers who cared, the mentors who helped them, the bosses who took them under their wing, and the parents who pushed them to do well, but also resolve to help the next group of people who are struggling. For the life of me, I don't understand those who fall into the former category, because the belief that they did it all on their own is just nonsense. Most people have somebody who helped them somewhere along the way, and yet some of them don't recognize that and feel no need to reciprocate.

The fact is, many people are poor due to neglect and lack of opportunities. Some of them have parents who are in jail or addicted to drugs, and all of those circumstances contribute to the conditions that mold them as they grow up. So, for me a big part of being a Democrat is speaking for the voiceless, helping the downtrodden, and trying to create a little more equity in this life so that people have access to the same opportunities.

After my first semester of law school, Loretta wanted to know how I'd been doing. Having just taken the exams, I was not feeling superconfident about my grades, and she was really beating up on me: "Did you score well on all your tests? You need to be in the top ten percent of your class." She was applying all this pressure, and so I said, "I don't know how I did, Loretta. I tried, but it was really tough, and the entire semester has been extremely hard."

Well, she wasn't taking any excuses. "If you're not in the top ten percent of your class," she warned me, "you won't be able to get a good corporate legal job."

I looked at her in complete disbelief. "What makes you think I want to do corporate law? I want to do legal services. I want to work for the United Farm Workers."

Now she was shocked. Loretta had already helped me quite a lot in terms of mentoring me and encouraging me to go to law school, but she'd also assumed that what she wanted for me was what I wanted for me. My reaction was "Wait a minute, when did I ever give you that impression?"

It was like this moment of complete shock and disbelief on both our parts, and she was really taken aback: "Why would you put yourself through all this to go work somewhere that pays you twenty-six thousand a year?"

"I just want to help people," I replied. "That's why I went to law school. I didn't come here to make as much money as possible working eighty hours a week for some large corporation. That was never my intention."

When I finally graduated and passed the bar, I went to work for a firm that handled a lot of migrant farmworker cases—ones pertaining to their being horribly maimed or killed because of people's negligence or even gross negligence. I really loved that work. While there, I had experiences that shaped me forever. For example, there was one case where workers being transported from one field to another had traveled in the back of a tractor trailer. No seats, no seat belts, nothing. Well, the truck had become involved in an accident and went up in flames, and because no one could open the rear door several people were severely injured; some even died. Just gruesome. It was as if these people were expendable and their lives were of no value. I never wanted to see another human suffer this way, and to this day I fight to prevent that kind of cruelty.

Having the courage of your convictions—that is tested a lot in the Congress. I sometimes get disappointed by colleagues who either cave in or trade away their values in exchange for something else. Horse trading goes on here, and you expect that to some degree, but not on certain key issues. Like Loretta, I'm not paranoid about losing office, and so there's no need for me to compromise my values. I'm only in my late thirties, and so if tomorrow I wasn't reelected there would still be many other things I could do and probably be happy doing. My identity is not just as a member of Congress.

I think the longer you stick around this place, the more who you are as a person gets wrapped up in your title. And if you lose that title, you lose your sense of who you are. Whereas some members will stay in Congress until the bitter end, I don't see myself as one of those who'll have to be carried out feetfirst in a box. There is something to be said for new ideas and passing the torch. And when you get jaded and cynical and trade away all your values, you don't belong here anymore. I have a very strong sense of what I stand for, and I don't veer from that. But if there ever comes a day when I vote according to my convictions and my constituents don't like it and don't reelect me, well then, maybe I'm just not a good fit for that constituency anymore.

I regret very few votes that I've ever taken, but I can think of one major exception. After Janet Jackson's "wardrobe malfunction," when her breast made an appearance during the 2004 Super Bowl half-time show, Congress wanted to pass a super strict bill that would fine artists $500,000 for such behavior, as well as the TV channels that broadcast it during prime time.

This was an overreaction, in my opinion, and it resulted in a bill with really, really onerous penalties. I have a hard time imagining that, given the distances, everybody in that football stadium saw Jackson's breast. The photos that appeared on the Internet caused most of the furor, with adults mostly initiating the discussions that led to the full-blown scandal: "Children could have been watching!" I don't doubt that children could and might have caught a glimpse, but I really don't think exposure to the bared breast for a nanosecond would mentally traumatize them for the rest of their lives. Nevertheless, there was all this fuss and members began receiving phone calls, letters, and e-mails about the moral corruption of our society.

I would agree that, until then, the fines for such on-air incidents were ridiculously low, but what Congress did was write a bill that would fine the artist hundreds of thousands of dollars for each news outlet on which it played. For an event as large as the Super Bowl, that would run into the millions, and what's more, the broadcast channels would be fined $500,000 as well. Bankruptcy over a bare breast? Maybe not, but the sums were really exorbitant. At the same time, we were under a lot of pressure from our constituents, many of whom were demanding stronger action to protect our children, and at the end of the day, concerned that the existing fines were too low, I voted for the bill.

When I walked out of the chamber, I just didn't feel right. Yes, the penalties needed to be harsher, but this was an overreaction and it niggled at me. For the next few days, it kept popping into my mind, and I had this terrible feeling that I'd done the wrong thing. Fortunately, I was able to go back and make it right. The bill never cleared both Houses, and so when it was reintroduced at the next congressional session, I had the opportunity to cast another vote, and this time around I was one of about thirty members who voted against it. That meant it was passed, but at least I felt like I had done the right thing.

Of course, there are times when speaking out and going against the grain ends up getting you into trouble—which has happened to me more times than I can count—and so you have to be strategic about when you choose to stand up for your convictions. However, a life in which the only way to get along is to swallow your convictions is no life at all. You have to be comfortable with where you live and work, or else you'll be miserable. And if something bothers you, then speak out about it. No one wants to lose his or her job, but if that's what happens as a consequence of your being true to your beliefs, my guess is you'll probably end up finding something that you prefer doing, or a place that respects you and shares your own values.

# 6

# No Woman Is an Island

People who try to succeed on their own within any given field often work harder than they have to and probably accomplish a lot less than they otherwise could. In our experience, partnering with others is an absolute necessity. These others could be members of your family, union, staff, or political party; friends, constituents, or individuals in positions of influence; or simply Blue Dog Democrats. They could even be– *gasp, slapping our foreheads*–Republicans!

Our teaming experiences have invariably enhanced our ability to translate convictions into concrete results, whether these have pertained to fending off the prolonged and costly attacks of a livid political opponent or reversing the declining trend in trade union membership. And they have also taught us about the art of compromise when trying to achieve a common goal.

## LORETTA

Halloween has always been widely celebrated in Anaheim, California, and I just loved it when I was growing up. The merchants would decorate their places of business, the City Hall would be turned into a haunted house that we could visit in order to be scared out of our wits, and those of us in first through ninth grades would all don costumes on the Friday morning immediately preceding the holiday weekend and march in the kiddie parade. Then, on the Saturday night, there would be an even larger parade, featuring floats, high school bands, and plenty of decorations. It was a really big deal.

One year, Mom decided the theme for our costumes should be *The Wizard of Oz*. I was cast as Dorothy, my older brother Henry was the Scarecrow, our younger brother Frank was the Cowardly Lion, our sister Martha was Glinda, and then Mom began using neighborhood kids from across the street. Dad turned one girl into the Tin Man and another into the Wicked Witch of the West, and there were also tons of little Munchkins. Everyone collaborated, and so when we turned up for the Friday morning parade and a panel of judges wanted to hand best-costume prizes to the Scarecrow and the Tin Man, my mother said, "No, this is a total outfit."

The whole neighborhood had been involved, and instead of marching with each of our classmates, we had switched the rules on everybody by marching together, just behind the school banner. Mom therefore pointed to us and said, "You give one a prize, you give all of them a prize," and as a result we all got Disneyland tickets. Then and there, I recognized the power of collaboration. Yet, I also took it for granted, since working together and assisting one another was characteristic of not only my family, but also the Hispanic culture.

In Washington, it's a different matter. There, my colleagues are so busy, they may not even notice I'm trying to get something done. Yet, that doesn't mean they don't want to help. In fact, I believe most people do want to help. After all, when you ask for that, people are usually flattered. The problem is, they either don't know you need help or don't know *how* to help you. That's why you have to ask for their help, let them know what you're trying to accomplish, and provide them with a concrete list of things they can do. It often pays to find out about a person's experience and abilities, so that if you ever need a certain skill set, you'll know whom to ask.

I remember when the Republicans controlled the Congress, a Latina Democratic colleague from California asked me, "Why are you talking to *Republicans*?" Having come from a state legislature that was completely controlled by Democrats, she had never needed to work with Republicans. I told her, "That's just not how it works here. If you don't talk to Republicans, you won't get anything done." Still, it took her about eight months to fully accept that there are many areas where we transcend our differences.

For example, Tom Tancredo, a representative from Colorado, takes a hard-line stance against immigration that I truly do not believe in, yet he and I coauthored a bill legislating loan forgiveness for nurses, because we both recognized the need for more nurses in the system. People kept asking me, "How can you even *talk* to Tancredo?" and I would say, "Why? When I talk to him, it's about *medical care*. It has nothing to *do* with immigration." And that's very easy for me.

When my colleagues have gone on television to debate him on immigration, there have been some pretty heavy altercations. Often their differences are so dramatic that they are in separate studios. However, many times when Tancredo and I have gone on TV to debate immigration, he and I have been side by side in the same room. We've clearly had opposing views on some things, on others we've agreed, and along with some kidding we've actually had a good time. And that's because, as much as we've been discussing a serious issue, it doesn't mean I can't talk or stand up to him or even accept the validity of some of the things that he says.

The same has applied to my human rights work, which I do with many Republicans who, again, don't see eye to eye with me on a number of issues. For example, Chris Smith of New Jersey is totally antichoice and yet he's a very staunch supporter of human rights. He and I have worked on those issues as they pertain to Vietnam, getting it listed among the countries that are of particular concern with respect to religious freedom. That's a big deal, and I couldn't have done it without the support of both Chris and the president.

Between 2004 and 2006, I was denied access to Vietnam three times, having requested to go there to talk with government staff. Vietnam is a Communist country that, in my view, treats many of its people like garbage. I'd gone there a couple of times before and talked with dissidents about how we might get the government to change its policies. The last occasion had been in 2000, when I'd visited there with President Clinton and staged a summit of six major human rights activists who'd previously never been allowed to meet each other. Without anyone else's knowledge, we'd been able to get them together in the same room, and this had made headlines, infuriated the authorities, and subsequently led to their not granting me a visa when I asked to return. They didn't call me a terrorist—they stopped just short of that—but Vietnam's National Assembly simply voted against my being allowed back into the country.

I told a Democratic comrade of mine, Solomon Ortiz, who's a chairman on the Military Committee, that I was organizing an official trip to Vietnam and that ultimately I wanted him to take it over. If someone more senior in authority decides to go on such a trip, it becomes his or her trip, and so I wanted this to be "Congressional Delegation Ortiz" instead of "Congressional Delegation Loretta Sánchez." My desire was to get into Vietnam for the purpose of promoting human rights, and with his cooperation I achieved that in April 2007. After all, Vietnam wants to talk about forging military ties with the United States and getting equipment from us, and here was the chairman from the Military Committee asking for a meeting. Of course, when he submitted a list of delegates that included my name, Mr. Ortiz also had to make all kinds of promises about my behaving. In the end they appoved my entry visa, which, I admit, surprised me.

After we arrived there, I did whatever was required of me as part of the Ortiz group. However, I had also spoken with the U.S. ambassador to Vietnam, and he had set up a tea with the wives and mothers of political prisoners. Prisoners of conscience now number in the thousands. Since January 2006, anyone who talked publicly about having a more open government or free elections had been thrown in jail, and so there were no dissidents for me to meet, only their relatives. Ambassador Marine therefore organized a tea at his residence for them to express their concerns. They didn't know where the prisoners were or what conditions they were living in, so he arranged for us to meet them *and* he told the Vietnamese government that he was going to do this.

In the hours leading up to the five o'clock meeting, I was informed that many of the women were being arrested while trying to leave their homes or were being detained at their homes or in local police precincts. The surrounding streets had all been cordoned off, and so I arrived for the meeting knowing that probably no one was going to show up. Nevertheless, two other women did get there at five o'clock, and as we were about to enter Ambassador Marine's compound about twenty-five Vietnamese police and army personnel descended upon us. While dragging one of the women away they got into an altercation with me and the other woman, and when the ambassador tried to intervene he was brushed aside. My military escort got everything on video; we were able to smuggle it out of the country and it became an international incident. After all, you just don't treat people like that, whether they're older women or younger congresswomen.

None of us were protected in that situation. The Vietnamese police and military could easily have harmed us. When you're in a foreign country you are subject to its laws, unless you have a diplomatic passport. I was therefore taking my life into my own hands, but at least I got there, and that was thanks to the assistance of Congressman Soloman Ortiz, not to mention that of Ambassador Marine in terms of bringing attention to our cause.

The video that we smuggled out appeared on YouTube, and the next day U.S. Secretary of State Condoleeza Rice made a public statement about how the ambassador and I had been treated. She then dispatched her assistant secretary of state for Asian Affairs to Vietnam, asking to see some of the dissidents within the prison system, and although Vietnamese government officials said we couldn't tell them what to do on their sovereign territory, the condemnation by the U.S. secretary of state did have some effect. The Vietnamese president was scheduled to visit the United States several months later, and because of what had happened our president informed him that, instead of staying at Blair House—opposite the West Wing of the White House—like all other heads of state, he would have to stay at a hotel, which is what he did.

On the House floor, many of my colleagues commented that they hadn't realized I work so hard on human rights, and that it really was a badge of honor to have done what I did. I was subsequently asked to testify before the International Relations Committee when it held a hearing on the treatment of prisoners of conscience in Vietnam, and then Bill Delahunt, the chairman of the subcommittee that deals with Vietnam, asked me to be present when a Vietnamese delegation was visiting. Once again, he brought up the whole issue of not treating a congresswoman the way they had treated Congresswoman Loretta Sánchez, and that has continued to reverberate as we go forward in our relationship with Vietnam.

I would like to think that human rights is a nonpartisan arena, yet you still have to work with people who are often very opposed to the other things you do and stand for. Chris Smith and I push our joint agenda by putting together an annual human rights hearing. And while I probably wouldn't work with someone whom I regard as completely reprehensible, so far I haven't been put to that test. I'll generally work with anybody to get the job done.

Sitting as the chairwoman of the Border Security Committee, I've watched everybody in the Congress become a border expert. It's one of the hottest topics right now. At one Blue Dog meeting, a young freshman Democrat turned up and announced that, like virtually everyone else, he had his own border bill. "It's not about amnesty or housing illegal immigrants," he declared. "It's about more border patrol and closing off the borders to stop these people coming in."

This prompted quite a debate. However, when I raised my hand to speak, the man who was running the meeting informed me that we'd gone way overtime. "We'll listen to you later, Loretta," he said, to which I replied, "No, you'll listen to me *now*." It was clear that he wanted to end the debate and move on to something else because the whole thing had gotten out of hand, but I was a little testy about it.

"If any of you have border bills, you might want to come and talk to the *chairman* of the Border Security Committee. That, by the way, would be *me*. And since any bill you do has to go through me, it really might help to consider my involvement. After all, you may think many of the things you put in there are really smart, but they may not be so smart, and so you might come and ask me or my committee staff about what we've already tried and whether or not it's succeeded."

At this point, the freshman got a little bent out of shape, arguing again the merits of the bill and instructing me to support it.

"I take a look at all the bills," I told him, "and I think we may pass something this year."

"Well, maybe we'll pass my bill," he said, to which I responded, "Don't you count on that!"

You have to think about what you're doing. When I wanted to do the bill on the military rape law I asked for dinner with the Armed Services Personnel Subcommittee chairman, John McHugh. If you're really going to spend a lot of time on a bill, then you need to get the right person on your side from the very beginning. And for that to happen, you often have to know how to compromise. Two people may have all the same objectives with regard to a particular issue, but if both of them go off and write bills without ever speaking to one another the bills are going to look significantly different.

When I'm at fund-raisers or at town hall meetings, I always tell people "When you put me here, there's only one person who thinks the votes I'm casting are one hundred percent right, and that's *me*. You're never going to have the perfect person casting the perfect vote. The reason you vote for me is because you really don't want to do this job for one hundred and sixty thousand dollars a year—you don't want to keep flying back and forth, you don't want to put up with the public scrutiny, you don't want to work seven days a week. So, you send Loretta instead. However, when you send Loretta, you do so understanding she's not going to vote one hundred percent like you."

It's a compromise every single time with every bill on the floor, unless it's my bill and it hasn't been amended. Take the debate over whether people can be dismissed from their jobs simply because they're gay or lesbian. There are thirty states where that is legal, but many would like to pass a federal law that would prohibit this. There's also a question as to whether or not transgender people should be similarly protected. According to true constitutional rights, of course they should be, but this creates a whole new issue. There are two openly gay people in the Congress—Barney Frank and Tammy Baldwin—and Barney has said that since there are enough votes to pass a bill relating to gays and lesbians, let's just do that. Tammy, on the other hand, has stated that we also need to include transgender people, and so there's a big fight over what the Democrats should be trying to do.

The problem is, if I vote for a bill that protects only gays and lesbians, then I appear not to support transgender people. But if I vote for a bill that does include transgenders, I may torpedo the only chance for gays and lesbians to get equal rights. It's a no-win situation, and these are the types of issues that we face every day. So again, it's about compromise, and there are times when doing so has led me to feel like I've also compromised my beliefs. Still, if I walk out of the chamber and don't feel good after casting a vote, I usually turn around, go back, and change it.

Part of mastering the art of compromise is realizing the few times it is not an option. With big votes there can be no compromise. The war is the war, and if you're going to send kids to war, you must be 100 percent sure of your reasons. But other than these crucial issues, many smaller votes can go one way or the other without dire consequences.

## LINDA

When I was growing up, my older brothers and sisters were generally available when I needed help with homework, sports, you name it. At least one of them would have the relevant knowledge or experience, which was tremendously useful, and when it came to baseball we could field almost an entire team, visiting the park with Dad to practice throwing to first base, making outs, etc. So, especially as one of the younger siblings, I definitely saw the value in consulting and collaborating with others, even if I took it for granted.

Having played a lot of sports, I've always been a real believer in teamwork. I didn't really participate in what I consider to be highly individualized activities, such as tennis or golf. For me, it was much more fun being with a group of people who were all working toward the same goal, and at school I also loved projects where I got to collaborate with my classmates. Later on, at college, for some of the more challenging classes we'd break up into study groups, and I had a really good friend there who, rather than read the material, preferred to sit in on the group to reap the benefit of our collective knowledge. At a certain point, I realized this person wasn't pulling her weight and wasn't contributing, and that really bothered me. If you're going to work together with other people, you'll have to pull your own weight and contribute. Because if everybody does that, you will cover so much more ground.

When I was elected to run the Central Labor Council, I attended AFL conferences to learn about how to help local unions organize other workers and win contracts, and I asked more seasoned leaders of CLCs around the country, "Wow, how did you guys manage to organize the workers in your county?" They told me they went to the Interfaith Committee for Worker Justice (ICWJ) and got the clergy and people of faith to support their organizing efforts so that the workers wouldn't be scared but would understand this was about dignity and a living wage. They also recruited the help of the Coalition of Labor Union Women (CLUW) and the LCLAA, a Latino labor organization, and then they wrote out a plan of action and went with that.

As I listened to this, I knew Orange County didn't have a CLUW chapter or a chapter of the Interfaith Committee for Worker Justice, or indeed any of the component parts that you need for a successful organizing campaign. I felt like I was in the desert without a camel or water, and I wondered what I was going to do, before telling myself, "We'd better build those component parts." And that's exactly what I did, helping to set up our first ever local chapter of the Interfaith Committee, and gathering people of different faiths—rabbis, imams, Catholic priests, and others—to talk about the injustice in terms of the conditions for some of these workers. We also created a local CLUW chapter, and while it took months to do these things, the component parts enabled us to have very successful organizing campaigns in Orange County while I was there.

People initially told me, "You'll never organize janitors in Orange County. Orange County is too conservative," and "You'll never get a contract for the in-home health workers," but we achieved both of those things, and that was amazing. It was a team effort, courtesy of all the aforementioned organizations coming together, along with human rights groups and various other really great associations that joined with us.

When I landed in Washington, it was with a little bit of fanfare due to Loretta's and my being the first sisters in Congress, and I guess I expected other members—especially the female ones—to take me under their wing, show me the ropes, and acclimate me to D.C. However, that really didn't happen, and I didn't know why. Maybe they figured Loretta would be doing all of that for me. And she did, in terms of helping me to get set up, though she and I didn't serve on the same committees.

I assumed that some of the more senior members would help me, too. That was, until I learned that everybody in Washington is busy and nobody just stops what they're doing to help people. If you approach people and ask for their help, that's a different matter—they're more than willing—and so instead of waiting for them to come to you, you have to be proactive and seek them out. I don't always find it easy to ask for assistance, but once I figured out what to do and did approach certain members, they were extremely helpful.

In Washington, loyalty is the most precious commodity...

next to information. Information is power, but loyalty runs a close second, and it is very hard to come by. In fact, I learned that early on with regard to the people who are hired to assist and support me. About eight of them are based in my Washington office, another eight are in my district office, and at one point I allowed a senior member of my staff to do the interviewing because I was busy. Well, she began hiring friends of hers—and friends of friends—who consequently felt beholden to her rather than loyal to me, the member of Congress. That led to problems—certain employees were treated better than others in terms of bonuses and days off, and I didn't become aware of that until it was too late, at which point I basically had to clean house.

I had to let three or four people go within the space of two weeks, because the whole thing was infecting the office and I needed a fresh start. Since then, I've handpicked everyone who works for me, and when people turn up for interviews I tell them, "I'm not just looking for those who have the education and the experience and are competent. I'm also looking for people whose attitude matches that of the office. In my office everybody pitches in when there's work to be done, and all of us help each other out so that no one person is burning the midnight oil." It's very important to me that their personality and their attitude reflect that team spirit.

The district office represents my public face because the people there interact with those who elect me. They're the ones who represent me at district events when I'm voting or doing legislative work in Washington, and that means they must have really great personal skills. They have to be accessible, they have to be helpful, and they have to deliver. If individual constituents come in with problems, my staff members must be responsive and try to resolve those issues satisfactorily and as quickly as possible. And if they're asked to speak or hand out an award at a community event that I can't attend, then they also have to serve as my voice.

The Washington office is more about the inner workings of policy and legislation. The people there do research on the different bills, they keep me prepared for hearings, and overall I see them as sifters and condensers. They take a lot of information and boil it down to the essential substance— "Here is what you need to know about this issue, and these are the different perspectives on how to solve this problem. One side says this, the other side says that."

Again, teamwork is the key, and both offices interact with one another. Often, there will be training sessions in Washington, D.C., and the district office staff will go there to learn about topics relating to social security, perhaps, or how to deal with veterans' health care issues. Then, at the start of each two-year congressional cycle, we have a retreat at which there are joint planning sessions about our goals and expectations for the year, and the location for this alternates between the district and D.C.

What we try to create is a synergy and an understanding

between the two offices, because everybody's role is important. You must have faith and confidence in whom you select to manage your district office and whom you select as your chief of staff. And I'm very fortunate because the teams I have in place now work tremendously well together. Their styles are probably a little bit different from mine, but they communicate with me as often as possible. So, even when I'm not in the district office, I'm constantly receiving e-mails and text messages on my BlackBerry phone about things that are happening or decisions that need to be made. And for my part, I also try to communicate with my staff as much as I can.

There are some offices where members don't carry cell phones, and when they're gone everyone else is scrambling around because they need an answer or they need information. The reason I know that? I've actually had other offices call me to ask where a particular member is! I'm generally always accessible. My staff members know where I am almost every minute of every day.

When it comes to the House, you often find unusual allies—members whom you do not agree with on one issue, yet with whom you may be in complete agreement on another. So, you take allies where you can find them, and while working with someone whose ethics are contrary to your own is not easy, you learn to do it. When I first entered the Congress as a freshman, I'd think, "Oh my God, I'd never want to work with those people," but as I gained experience in D.C., I came to realize that you don't need to agree 100 percent with everybody you're working with. In fact, if that's what you're looking for, you're not going to be working with anybody but yourself.

That having been said, there are also times when you're expecting help or support for something—even within your own caucus—and it isn't forthcoming. Often you can't figure out why, but quite frankly it's not unusual for this to be based on conflicting personalities. And it can also be due to someone playing politics and just trying to place you in an awkward position. On occasion, when I'm trying to move a bill and meeting resistance from an assumed ally, especially a Democratic colleague, I'll joke to myself, playing with Perry's famous words, "I have met the enemy, and they are us." Sometimes the people who are serving as the biggest opponents and throwing up the biggest obstacles are the ones who should be helping you.

Then, of course, there's the old adage, "My enemy's enemy is my friend." In this instance, *enemy* is probably too strong a word, but the saying does come into context regarding the elections for leadership positions within our caucus—for the speaker, the majority leader, the whip, the chair, and the vice chair. Sometimes three candidates will be vying for a slot, and so there will be an initial ballot to eliminate one of them. Once that happens, the supporters of the losing candidate will then team up with the supporters of one of the other candidates in order to gang up on the third candidate. A case of one candidate's attracting not only his own supporters, but also those who view him as the proverbial lesser of the evils.

Like the Democratic caucus, the congressional Hispanic caucus (CHC) also has elected leaders. Loretta and I no longer belong to the Hispanic caucus, but that's where, as a woman, I've certainly experienced a lack of support. In 2006, Joe Baca was running for chairman—an older member who has made some very disparaging remarks to me about women, and about Latina women in particular. Male superiority is very deeply ingrained in some Latino men of a certain generation—the old "women should be seen and not heard" philosophy—and Baca belongs to that camp, although he would certainly deny that.

With a whole cabal of males backing him up, he ended up getting elected, and this proved to be very divisive. I just didn't think his leadership style was inclusive, and he knew this. Loretta and I were suggesting changes to some of the bylaws and some of the structure of the caucus, which was very heavily weighted in terms of seniority—in other words, to the advantage of the males, since the first Latina wasn't elected until just over fifteen years ago. We wanted a more inclusive structure so that women could participate in a meaningful way, and it was clear to us some of the more senior members didn't like it.

When Baca learned that Loretta and I, along with another female member, weren't supporting his sons,

Jeremy and Joe Jr., in their run for State Assembly and State Senate, that made him mad. And we in turn learned that, at an event with Latino state legislators, he called Loretta "a whore." When I confronted Baca about this, he tried to placate me by saying he'd never made any such remark about me, just about Loretta! And when confronted about this in the press, he denied saying it altogether and refused to apologize. So, Loretta resigned from the congressional Hispanic caucus.

I followed suit a short time later, citing a need for structural reforms to ensure the caucus is more equitable and inclusive of all its members. The women within the CHC work really hard, and they're the ones who devote a lot of energy to advancing a positive agenda. Still, heaven forbid that the younger women who came in and worked their butts off should get any credit for doing this. Instead, our ideas and work were often minimized or ignored, and I eventually reached the point where I no longer felt it was worthwhile for me to associate with a group of people who should be our natural allies, yet have to struggle with all the obstacles they put in our path. Especially when I could be working with other members in the Democratic caucus who are genuinely interested in helping me make my legislation become law, and can also help me get the support that I need without my having to bang my head against the wall.

Of course, compromise is a reality in Washington, and you have to accept that you're never going to get 100 percent of what you want. When you're voting on legislation, you try to get as much good as you can, but you have to look at things on balance, and there are times when a bill *is* pretty evenly balanced. There's some good and some bad; you have to figure out which outweighs the other, and sometimes you have to hold your nose and vote for something. After all, even if the bill stinks and it's not what you really want, it may advance you a step further in the right direction or get you incremental changes that represent at least a slight improvement on what's gone before.

In 2007, we introduced a bill that would expand funding for the State Children's Health Insurance Program (SCHIP) from an annual average of $5 billion to $12 billion over the next five years. SCHIP is for families who earn too much money to qualify for Medicaid yet can't afford private health insurance for their kids, and a significant number of people in my district are eligible for that program and use it right now. The bill that the Democrats passed and which the president subsequently vetoed would have excluded from coverage children who are legal permanent residents but not U.S. citizens, and I had a really big issue with that.

Sickness doesn't only apply to those who have legal status. And if children are sick and they're going to school, they risk infecting other children. So, why we wouldn't want them to have access to health care if they're legally in the United States is beyond me. Some groups urged me not to support the bill because those children were excluded. But on balance, when I looked at how many children in my district are getting the coverage and all the families taking advantage of that program, I decided that not voting for the bill—and thereby also preventing *those* children from getting health coverage—would do more harm than good.

Sometimes, it's not the perfect bill and you agonize over that, and so you have to take the incremental change.

# 7

# Staying Power

The interrelated attributes of persistence and consistency have certainly both served us well. Sample our old-fashioned, door-to-door precinct walking to get elected and securing fourteen tickets for the congressional swearing-in ceremony when each representative is allotted only one: Linda helping one of the small cities she represents by securing long-needed funds to repair its major street after only six weeks in Congress; and Loretta bouncing back from a failed city council election by running for Congress.

Occasional failure and rejection are inevitable side effects when taking risks, but these quickly become dusty memories so long as you refuse to accept defeat and just keep on trying.

## LORETTA

At one time, our father was a ballplayer back in Mexico, and when we were growing up he'd always apply the art of baseball to everyday life. He would attend our league ball games and take notes on what we did wrong when we were fielding a ground ball or striking out, and then during Sunday practice sessions in the park he would try to correct our mistakes: "You need to keep your eye on the ball to stop it going through your legs," or "Shorten your swing when you're down two strikes," that kind of thing. He would practice over and over with us until he felt we'd gotten the message, and then he would attend the next game that one of us played to see if what he taught was being implemented.

This is how Dad went about everything. If any of us had a problem with one of our school activities, he'd ensure that we worked on it until we conquered our fears and got it right. "You must never give up," he would always say, and that was his way of motivating us, particularly with sports, and so we learned that in order to be good you have to recognize your mistakes, learn from them, practice doing things the right way, and just keep at it. Dad didn't want us to overdo things to the point of injuring ourselves, but he always believed that we had talent, and that it wasn't due to lack of talent that we weren't getting something done. It was simply because we had to learn a different way of doing something, and he absolutely knew that, with sufficient effort and the right kind of application, we could do it. And he was right. I had to believe that I could achieve anything if I made the right adjustments and put in the effort, and that has proven to be true. During the early nineties, when I was living on my own in Anaheim, I kept bugging my longtime friend, Mayor Tom Daly, about some of the finance bills that the city was passing. Of course, I was a securities advisor, and so I'd complain about this and that until finally he turned to me one day and said, "You need to run for the city council."

"Nah," I said, "I don't want to do that."

Now it was his turn to bug me, and he kept bugging and bugging and bugging me, and I kept waiting and waiting and waiting, and by the time I entered the race in April 1994 it was clear that I had waited too long. There were other people in the race, I didn't know the importance of raising money, and once I did start raising money I didn't raise it fast enough. What's more, although the city council race is nonpartisan, as a county Orange County is very partisan. The Republicans don't like the Democrats at any level, especially Democrats they don't already know. So, about two weeks before the November election they saw my name and began asking, "Who is she? Where's she from?"

Soon they found out: I was from Anaheim, I had

walked door-to-door every day with my husband, and everyone there knew me and my family. During the last week of the election there was a big push by the Republican Party to assert that Loretta Sánchez is basically Bill Clinton and that people shouldn't vote for a Democrat. Which is essentially what happened—I lost and it was hard to take. For one thing, I wasn't partisan, and so I was asking, "Why would they do that?" Tom Daly replied, "Because they're afraid of you."

Here I was, new, ambitious, and according to the poll numbers, making a good impression on voters. My popularity meant I was a threat to the status quo, and the Republicans in control didn't want that. But I was okay with that. After all, I had run a good race. I had met people, I had raised money, I had held my own in debates, I had walked door-to-door, and I had enjoyed the whole process. So, although I wasn't thrilled with the result, I knew I could hold my head high, and a lot of people told me that, including several Republicans.

For me, bouncing back from that defeat wasn't so difficult. In fact, while all the Democrats were so depressed—this was the year they lost the House, they lost everything—I didn't even know what that meant. Now I understand the significance of losing control of the House of Representatives but back then I wasn't a politician. So, when I saw all these depressed people, I wondered, "What's *their* problem?" Besides, I soon had my mind on a bigger goal. After my encounter with Bob Dornan got me mad a year later, I went to my lawyer and friend Wylie Aitken and told him, "I want to run again in an election." "Great," he said, "we'll be ready to support you again for the council," to which I responded, "No, no, I'm now running for Congress."

"Let me get this straight," Wylie remarked. "You run for city council and you lose, so now you're going to run for Congress. If you lose for Congress will you run for the Senate?"

"Maybe, Wylie. In the meantime, may I count on your support?"

He said, "I may be crazy, but I'll support you," and he subsequently served as the chairman of my first congressional campaign.

This again saw my husband and me walking door-to-door every single day for a year. Sometimes it would be 102 degrees outside, and when people opened their doors, the cool air from their air-conditioning wafting out, they'd say, "Are you *crazy*? Do you know how *hot* it is out there? Why are you doing this?" I'd tell them there was no other way I was going to familiarize myself with the voters.

I filed papers to run for Congress on December 11, 1995, and the election took place on November 5, 1996. While I enjoyed campaigning, there were days when, like anyone else, I would return home exhausted and think,

"Oh man, I don't know if I can go back out and do this." Nevertheless, I did. And if I had to walk door-to-door at night and I told my husband, "I can't walk out there by myself," he'd go too. He walked every single day with me, and we'd even knock on separate doors to cover more ground.

Sometimes it would be getting dark and there might be five more houses left on the block, and even if I was really tired I would always say to myself, "Without these five houses I might lose by five votes." I'm very disciplined and self-motivated. Dad used to say, "With whatever you do, you must have a plan." If I've got a goal and my plan for reaching it includes walking that neighborhood, then I'm going to be out in that neighborhood, and I'm still that way. I continue to walk door-to-door when I'm campaigning, and if I'm tired before I get to the end of the block I think, "You can't quit now. These people could be very important."

I won my first election by just 984 votes, a small margin in politics. So every house we went to really was important.

For the January 1997 swearing-in ceremony, I was allotted just one ticket, yet I needed fourteen to accommodate my parents and family members. So, I called the Sargeant of Arms and asked, "How do I get more tickets?" He said, "Well, you'll have to hit up some of the other members." The fact is, if people have been in the Congress ten years and had five swearing-ins, they don't necessarily feel the need to invite family or friends to witness the event. I therefore got on the phone and used all my powers of persuasion to convince my new colleagues—both Republicans and Democrats—to part with their tickets, and the result was that I actually succeeded in obtaining the requisite fourteen, which was no small feat, especially since I had a limited time to do so. And when Linda was elected six years later, I e-mailed her and told her to do the exact same thing.

During my first year on the Hill, I traveled cross-country on forty-seven weekends to meet with my constituents, and I still do that. The only exceptions are when I'm on vacation or part of an official delegation to another country. I head home all the time, first because my family's there, second because I prefer California to D.C., and third because I not only want to tell my constituents what I'm working on, but I also want to hear their concerns. Plus I love being with them.

All that traveling is very hard, believe me—I pack my bag Friday morning, fly to L.A. Friday afternoon, do a full day's work on Saturday, a full day's work on Sunday, get on the red-eye Sunday night, arrive back in Washington Monday morning, and then work there until Friday, when I repeat the same routine all over again. That's my life. And while I've done it since 1996, I'm not going to be in the House forever, so I'm making the most of it. My constituents have afforded me the privilege of serving them in the House of Representatives, and so I wake up every day thinking, "How can I make things better?"

Politics and persistence go hand in hand. You can work and work and work on something and get nowhere. What's more, no one will know how much work you've put in. The Security and Accountability for Every Port (SAFE Port) Act is a prime example. After the September 11, 2001, attacks, we went through this whole issue of protecting our country and identifying what else the terrorists were going to hit, and we ended up forming the Homeland Security Committee that I now sit on. Under that jurisdiction is the country's infrastructure, and this includes ports, which are also overseen by a subcommittee over which I preside.

One of the reasons I chose that was that I had been working on things with respect to the ports, in particular with Juanita Millender-McDonald, who represented the port area of Long Beach, California. Juanita wrote a bill and I had already introduced three other port-related bills, and so our Homeland Security Committee rolled all of those into one much larger bill that was passed in the House of Representatives. Then it was sent over to the Senate and nothing happened with it. That was, until the whole Dubai Ports World (DPW) controversy, when it emerged that six major U.S. seaports were going to be managed by DPW, a state-owned company in the United

Arab Emirates. The American public went crazy, and so the Senate decided to act, and the person who headed that committee was Susan Collins of Maine.

She introduced a ports bill that covered the same ground as our bill that the Senate had never done anything with. She then called Jane Harman, who's a member of our committee, and Jane took the bill and worked on it with Dan Lundgren, the Republican chairman of the subcommittee that oversees the ports—of which I was the top Democrat. They put their names on the bill and it ended up being adopted, and that was interesting because it was essentially the same bill that Juanita and I had worked on for three or four years. Everyone on the committee knew this—the chairman acknowledged the work that the two of us had done—but the reality is that the time has to be right for things to happen.

The comprehensive immigration bill is a similar example. Lots of time and energy put into that, and it never even made it to the House. I worked on that for six years, trying to find compromises, and all for nothing. In my opinion, there are three aspects to dealing with immigration. First, we should have control over who goes in and out of our country. That's called border security, it includes all of our borders, and it goes under my committee. Second, we need to decide what to do with the people who are already here but don't have the right documents to be here. That would fall under Linda's judiciary committee on immigration. And third, we have to figure out how easily people should be able to legally travel back and forth to work or to enter and become citizens. That also falls under the Judiciary Committee.

Well, we worked on this and we worked on that, and nothing came of it. Then, after a couple of months I was informed that people wanted a border security bill that would have to come out of my Homeland Security Committee. Well, why should we? Why suddenly do border security when there are already plenty of laws on the books that say we should build a virtual fence and utilize more resources? Some people were so up in arms, they wanted to build an actual fence, but that would not be as effective. I think we need to deal with all three aspects of the immigration issue. So, I went to the leadership and asked, "Is it true that you want to do a border bill?" and I was told they would build only a virtual fence — consisting simply of measures to control immigration — if my committee told them to, and if in exchange for that we could figure out how to widen the gates for people to legally cross the border.

There we were, gearing up again to introduce a new bill, before I was again told nothing would happen in the near future. It's like stop and start, stop and start — "Okay, let's go work on something else, because this has got to stay in the oven for a little while. It's not yet ready to be served."

Often we just have to focus on what we can get done right now. And in terms of the bigger picture we also have to figure out how we can get more Democrats, how we can get a veto-proof majority, and how we can get a new president.

## LINDA

In high school I studied chemistry, which paradoxically was not only one of the most interesting subjects I ever took, but also one of the hardest. I was not doing at all well in that class, and my parents were really worried because they thought it could ruin my chances of getting into college. So, we made an agreement with my friend Kim, who was failing Spanish but was the chemistry student of the year. Mom said, "You can come live with us for a week and we'll teach you all the Spanish you need to know if you tutor Linda in chemistry."

That whole week, nobody in our household spoke to Kim in anything but Spanish, and she in turn spent a lot of time working with me on my chemistry. She actually tutored me for the entire semester, and I ended up getting a C+ in our class, which I was ecstatic over. It was the first time in my life I'd really had to work that hard just to get a passing grade, and it was kind of humbling for someone who was used to doing well at school without having to put much effort into it. When you're younger and things come to you fairly easily, you don't have a lot of compassion for people who struggle. That was until I found myself in the same situation. At that point, an average grade was a really good accomplishment, and it was achieved by working harder than usual and not giving up.

When Mom studied to get her college degree, she had to be very persistent. Her studies didn't take place in the normal time frame, but she took the approach of making small and steady progress until eventually reaching her goal. Both she and Dad always taught us that we could achieve whatever we wanted to do in our life and whatever we wanted to be. We'd just have to work hard enough and long enough and not give up. I remember Dad once sitting us all down and saying, "I don't care what you are when you grow up. I don't care if you're a doctor or a scientist or a maid or a gardener"—which really shocked me, because our parents never advocated for us to be maids and gardeners—"but I'm just going to ask two things of you: whatever it is that you ultimately choose to do, do it to the best of your ability and take pride in your work; and second, earn an honest living."

Our parents had initially lived in really rough neighborhoods, and they had seen people get involved in drugs, gangs, and other illegal activities. So, it was very important to Dad that, no matter what we did, we chose something legit and gave it our best shot and took pride in our profession even if it wasn't widely respected. Over and over, he and Mom would tell us, "Whatever you want to be, it's tough. So, play by the rules and don't give up if it gets hard along the way."

I think about my mom a lot when I think about perseverance and tenacity. She really had to decode so much of another culture, and, again, that didn't come easily. She suffered failures and embarrassments along the way, as well as plenty of put-downs from other people, but she never let any of that break her spirit. And I'm sure her example rubbed off on me when I went to law school, which I found to be very difficult. Much as I did in my chemistry class I had to read everything two or three times and study like mad to make the grade.

Law school, you see, represented a very different way of thinking and looking at the world. It was almost like learning a new language. Many of my fellow students had parents and grandparents who were attorneys or judges, so they'd grown up speaking their language. My siblings and I didn't even *know* an attorney growing up. I don't think our parents used an attorney for anything.

Even though I had done well in school, I didn't have the best study habits, because just by sitting at lectures and taking notes I'd usually have all the material I needed for the tests. Then suddenly law school came along, and I discovered that each day builds on the concept you learned the day before, and if you don't do your homework one day, in no time at all you're really behind. It was a struggle for me to comprehend that and do well, and I found it really stressful and frustrating.

I mean, while I was holed up in my room, studying for

hours and hours, I had friends who would go to a concert the night before a test and then do really well. I had a friend who didn't even buy a study book until midsemester, who borrowed my notes because she hardly ever went to class, and she ended up doing better than I did. Her father had been an attorney, her grandfather had been a judge, and that was probably the first time in my life when I really, really felt like I had to be tenacious and not get discouraged.

It's hard to avoid getting down on yourself when you're used to being an A student and suddenly you're happy just getting C's. In fact, I remember going home during finals week of my very first semester, and when Dad caught sight of me he was concerned that I looked so ragged. I told him, "Dad, this is really tough! I'm really struggling." You've got to remember, both he and Mom were pinning a lot of hopes on my doing well at law school. It was a big deal for immigrant parents, who didn't enjoy the same opportunities as us, to have a son or daughter at law school or at med school. That was like the pinnacle of having made it, and so I felt obliged to live up to my family's expectations.

"I'm trying hard," I continued, "but I'm not doing as well as I should be, and I'm feeling all this pressure."

"Do you like it?" my father asked.

"Well, I like what I'm learning, Dad, but I don't like the way I'm being pushed to learn it."

"If you're not happy, you don't have to do it," he remarked.

It was shocking to me that Dad would even suggest giving up on something, but he continued by recalling how, when he first arrived in this country, long before he became an industrial mechanic, he'd worked as a car mechanic and had hated being in an enclosed space, underneath the vehicle. "I made good money at it, but I gave it up," he said. "At the time, my friends asked, 'Why are you giving up a good-paying job?' and I told them I was miserable. You don't have to do something if it makes you that unhappy."

Just his saying that really took a lot of pressure off me. It was like, "Okay, my father's not going to be disappointed if I don't finish law school." With that in mind, I went back and finished studying for my exams, all the time thinking, "Well, gee, I don't have to do this if I don't want to." Then I looked at my student loan debt and knew there was no way I couldn't finish. The sheer terror of how I was going to pay for that first year of law school really motivated me. I thought, "Screw that, I *have* to stay! Otherwise, I'll never be able to pay this off."

Still, it was nice knowing that, if I didn't want to continue, my whole family wouldn't feel disappointed in me. And with each semester, things became a little easier. In the end, my decision to tough it out really paid off, and although I never, ever thought I'd say this, I now actually look back on my years at law school with a little bit of nostalgia. At the time it was a living hell. It was probably the toughest thing I've ever done in my life, and that includes running for Congress.

When I had my first final exam in my first semester, I was nauseous. I wanted to go to the bathroom and throw up. I was *scared*. It seemed so hard, and I've never had that reaction to a test at any other time. It was humbling. I knew this was for real and I couldn't mess around. I was here and I had to do this. It's not like I was a terrible student at law school, but I was in the middle of the curve, and there's so much emphasis placed on being in the top 10 percent of your class or else you're never going to find a legal job.

There are a lot of mind games at law school, and a lot of pressure is applied to freak one another out, but I had a great teacher who told me that the people who do really well at law school are not always the ones who end up being the best attorneys. Sometimes, middle-of-the-curve students who end up with their own practices get a lot of attention for taking on novel, groundbreaking cases that perhaps the big firms wouldn't, and end up really distinguishing themselves professionally.

I never forgot what that teacher told me, and I held that belief close inside because I needed help, and it provided a little kernel of hope that, even though I wasn't in the top 10 percent of my law class, I could be successful nonetheless. The pressure to succeed was enormous, and the same applied when I ran for Congress. Initially a lot of people assumed that Loretta had just conscripted me. They were skeptical, and they'd dismiss me, thinking, "She's not talented, she's just Loretta's sister," or "She has nothing to offer, it's just a political move."

Other members of Congress have run their sons for Assembly seats in their congressional district, and, even in instances when the kids really don't have much to offer and have no business running for office, sometimes they win. It's pure nepotism, and so I think people were looking at me through the same lens. As a result, the pressure to win was absolutely huge—I wanted the chance to prove everyone wrong, but I'd have to work really hard to achieve that, and I'd be doing so in the full glare of the public spotlight. It's not as if I was going for a promotion within some firm. This was very high profile.

Campaigning is about tenacity. So, if you've never liked the idea of telemarketing or selling door-to-door, don't run for office, because you're going to call on people every day and ask them for money, or you're going to call on voters and ask them for their votes, and throughout that process you're going to experience plenty of rejection, with people hanging up on you or slamming the door in your face. Essentially, you're selling yourself as a candidate, and sometimes that serves as the perfect excuse for people to say nasty things or simply stop you dead in your tracks. It's not easy.

For all the pitfalls, I love old-fashioned door-to-door precinct walking. That's my favorite part of the campaign. It's like a psychology lesson. I mean, you walk up to a house, you look at it, and you try to guess what kind of person lives inside. You have minimal information from the voter role— it's a woman in her forties and she lives with one other registered voter. But the house itself gives you all kinds of clues as to the person's taste, personality, and lifestyle. Of course, toys in the front yard usually mean kids, while other telltale signs may indicate if the voter is a dog person or cat person. I'll try to get as much idea as I can before knocking on the front door and starting a conversation.

All of this came naturally to me during my first campaign, and so putting in all the hard work was actually more invigorating than tiring. It was like running the marathon—never give up, all the way to the finish line—and that turned out to be really good training for the persistence I'd need once I was elected. You see, members of Congress are like anybody else; they have bad days, and when you ask Democratic colleagues to help you with something or sponsor a bill, they might just say no, flat out. That, in turn, will make you feel a temporary sense of setback, but the next day you have to get up with renewed determination and maybe even re-approach the person who's just turned you down, even if you don't want to.

For me, it's hard with some of the more senior members whose time is extremely valuable. When I approach them I feel like I'm a kid tugging on their coat sleeves—"Please, please play with me." But I've got to do it. For instance, the Peru Free Trade Agreement was absolutely merciless work, because I was approaching colleagues not just once or twice, but three, four, five, six, seven times, urging them to vote against it, and it was rough going. When I'd first approach them, they might say, "Well, I don't know much about it," so I'd give them some initial information and be unsure as to whether they'd even read it or not. Next, I'd approach them and ask, "Did you take a look at the information?" only to hear, "Ah, I haven't had a chance," or "Oh, I gave it to staff."

So, then I would say, "Well, let me just tell you a little bit about why it's a bad idea," and I'd run through that really quickly because I might only have two or three minutes to do so. Regardless, they'd still be unsure about their position, so again I'd have to approach them and ask, "Have you given this more thought?"

"Yeah, but it looks like something I think I might be supporting."

Once more, I'd try to be persuasive, going back over some of the arguments to convince them to vote against the agreement while also remaining respectful of their opinions, and that could take a *lot* of time. Then again, sometimes I didn't even convince them, which meant I'd done all that work for nothing, and if that was the case I just had to move on. I may have lost the battle, but I couldn't give up on the war, and that's often the case in politics. You have to look at the big picture and accept the fact that achieving your goals may take a long, long time.

Shortly after entering the Congress I started work on a bill to resolve the situation where, if the police arrested undocumented immigrants on suspicion of major crimes and held them until their trial, a failure to convict would mean the local law enforcement would be responsible for the cost of housing them in the jails. That really should be the federal government's responsibility, because we are responsible for immigration enforcement. In a sense, the federal government had fallen down on the job and the state or local law enforcement had been picking up the tab. Before 1993, the federal government used to reimburse the cost of housing these criminal aliens regardless of whether or not they were convicted, but then the law was changed and that wasn't a smart move.

If the authorities arrested someone on suspicion of a crime but didn't have a rock-solid case, there was actually a disincentive to take that person into custody and formally charge him or her because they may never recoup the jail costs. That, in turn, increased the potential of criminals being out on the street, and so my bill would return things to how they were pre-1993—regardless of whether or not someone is ultimately convicted, if he or she is arrested and held for trial, the federal government will reimburse the local law enforcement. To do this, the bill inserted just three little words—*charged with or,* as in "anyone *charged with or* convicted of a crime"—yet the implications were huge, and I worked on this for many years.

Local law enforcement authorities were the ones who

originally came to me and said they really needed this, and I could definitely see why. State and local governments were losing a tremendous amount of money, and the other cockamamie thing about the 1993 change in the law was that, in addition to specifying people must be convicted in order for local law enforcement to be reimbursed their costs, those people also had to be convicted in the same year as their arrest! Therefore, if somebody robbed a house at Christmastime and was caught and imprisoned on December 26 but didn't go to trial until the end of January, then even if that individual was convicted the local authorities had to pick up the tab for his or her jail time. It was ridiculous.

It took until 2007 for the bill to finally be marked up in the immigration subcommittee, before being unanimously passed by the full House Judiciary Committee. One of the bill's cosponsors was Brian Bilbray, who's the head of this caucus on immigration reform that would like to shut down the border and build a wall with electrified fences, not to mention a moat with alligators. Bilbray was sensitive to the fact that the local law enforcement in his district was losing all the jail-related money that wasn't being reimbursed by the federal government, and so despite our opposing views on immigration, we were on the same page when it came to the bill. After all, the bill really wasn't about immigration policy, it was about fairness with regard to local and state law enforcement funding.

When I was first elected to Congress, I could tell that some of the local elected officials at the city level were not confident that I would be an effective member. I mean, I was the age of most of their children, had never held public office, and was in the minority party in Congress. Nevertheless, I took office determined to show them that although I might be young, I was there to do business, and I'd be around for a long time.

Before I even got sworn in, David Obey, the then-ranking member of the Appropriations Committee, called and told me that since some of the appropriations bills from the prior Congress had not been passed, an omnibus appropriations bill—meaning a year-end federal spending package—would be one of the first things that we would vote on after being sworn into Congress. Therefore, he advised me to have some projects ready, in the event that they could add them into the omnibus bill.

I represent several small cities that are always strapped for resources. So, taking the bull by the horns, I set up meetings with the city mayors and city managers from each city. At each meeting, I would ask the mayor and city manager about their priorities for their city in the upcoming year, and I would also ask them how I could help at the federal level. In many instances, I told them there would be federal funding opportunities as the appropriations process got under way.

One of the smaller cities I represent desperately needed funding to renovate and repave its major street, which was old and falling into disrepair. For ten years the city had been begging its former congressman to try to help it get federal funds for the roadwork, but he had never secured any real funding for the project. Well, when the time came, and Mr. Obey asked for projects, that was one of the projects I submitted. It made it into the omnibus bill, and the omnibus bill passed. That meant that after being in Congress for only six weeks, I was able to tell this city that I had gotten it the funding! And whereas before the city had been skeptical, I now had a victory to show them, and it was grateful.

Suddenly, people sat up and took notice. Here I was, a freshman in the minority, and I was producing for my constituents. Of course, none of this would have been possible if Mr. Obey had not been looking out for the freshmen and gone out of his way to help us, so for that I will always be grateful to him. But the other lesson that I learned was that because I took the time to meet with each city's leadership and listen to their needs, I was prepared to move quickly when the time came.

Every year, before the appropriations process begins, I schedule these meetings, and the cities I represent appreciate them tremendously. As a result, I have seen city leaders' attitudes about me change for the better. After two terms, I began getting endorsements from Republican city council members who have basically told me they may not agree with my positions on some issues, but I look out for, and take care of, my cities and they appreciate that. Proving I care and can deliver are things that, hopefully, constituents will value, and therefore convince them to keep me around for a long time.

It's important to pay attention to your moral compass and to stick to your guns on vital issues. However, that doesn't mean you can't be flexible. You might look at a piece of legislation, consider some new information, gain a fresh perspective, and change your position accordingly, and that's not necessarily a bad thing. So, while consistency is a virtue, this mainly applies to consistency in terms of the quality of your work and how you deal with your colleagues. I mean, there are days when I don't feel well because I've just gotten into town on a red-eye and I'm jet lagged, and it would be very easy to say, "I'm not coming into the office." But I have to be consistent. I have to show up for work, and even if I'm not feeling my best, try to bring my A-game.

Tenacity, reliability, consistency of effort—these are three key ingredients. And sometimes they are very difficult to sustain when whatever you do is deemed wrong and everyone is bearing down on you. Take immigration reform. While constituents might ask, "What have you been doing?" and "Why haven't you gotten it done?" there will be colleagues who are drafting immigration bills and trying to exclude me from the process, and leadership making the decision as to when a bill should be introduced. I don't control much of the process. I can do only so much, and so when my constituents start grilling me about what I've been doing with my time, it's often not easy to explain what went awry or why legislation is taking longer than expected.

When it comes to the war, many constituents are angry—they want us out of Iraq, and they'll ask when this is going to happen and why we haven't been able to force the issue. "I thought you guys were going to stand up to the president"—I hear that all the time and it's very hard to respond. People, ultimately, aren't interested in the interim steps, they're interested in the result, and when the result hasn't been achieved they don't think you've been doing your job. It's like attacking the waitress when the chef has screwed up your meal, or having a go at the attendant when a flight is delayed due to bad weather.

People often want answers to things that we can't predict and have no control over, and there are days when I go home and think, "Holy hell, everybody's angry at me. I'm trying my best!" Then there are the constituents who tell me how efficiently my office staff resolved a problem, or how much they appreciate the job that I'm doing on a certain issue. When I get those compliments, they mean that much more, because people usually find it far easier to criticize. And when they ask me why we haven't impeached President Bush, I say, "Do we really want Dick Cheney installed in the White House?"

"Well, no, no, no, impeach Cheney first."

"Oh, okay, let's impeach Dick Cheney. That'll take several months, and then we'll impeach Bush, which will take several more months. But who's the next person in line to take over as president when both of them are run out of office?"

"Nancy Pelosi!"

"Correct. So, we'll spend all this time to impeach Cheney and then Bush, just to have Nancy Pelosi be the president for five minutes before the next election. P.S. During the next presidential campaign, in every red state there will be ads about how the Democrats cheated and went after the president and vice president for political reasons so we could put our own person in the White House."

We're handcuffed. We don't have a veto-proof majority in Congress. If we did and the president vetoed our bills, we could override him in a heartbeat. We could have overridden the vote on the Iraq war and the timetable and the funding, as well as that on health care for poor children in this country. However, we don't have that many votes. Yes, we do have a majority, but we have to work with a president who is absolutely unwilling to compromise on *anything*. And believe me, being able to accept that takes a special kind of persistence and patience.

In the final analysis, the president is accountable to the people, and so there needs to be pressure around the country for his decisions on some of these bills. Sometimes when I'm asked, "What are you doing about this?" my response is, "Well, what are you doing about it? How about you applying pressure?" Once we pass a bill and send it to the president, our work is done. It's his turn now, and there needs to be pressure on the White House to do the right thing.

My California district is more Democrat than Republican, and the constituents there often forget that there are districts all over the United States where people don't think the way they do. In those districts the majority of constituents think Bush is doing a great job, and you're not going to get members of Congress to vote to override a veto on the SCHIP program if they don't think increasing the cigarette tax to fund children's health care is the right thing to do.

It can be frustrating, because we are doing our job. Watch C-Span, watch the hearings that we're conducting and the floor speeches that we're giving, denouncing the waste, fraud, and abuse in the Bush administration, along with all the politicization of government branches. This isn't carried on all the news outlets, because they're more interested in which celebrities have just gotten out of rehab. But we keep going regardless, and I do so by thinking about everything in terms of short-term and long-term strategy.

Sometimes you have to sacrifice the short-term strategy for the long-term strategy. It's not a sprint, it's a marathon. So, although you may not be running your fastest time in the first mile, if you're tenacious and you're determined and you're moving at a good clip, eventually you're going to win that race, because you'll have the energy to persevere throughout the twenty-six miles. That's the same with many things in life—it's about the marathon, not sprinting, and you don't want to start out full speed ahead, because that way you'll crash and burn. It's the long game, and you have to look at it in that perspective. We didn't get where we wanted in mile one, but we're going to get there eventually. And if it takes a little bit longer, then we're going to need a little more patience.

# 8

## Thick Skins Last Longer

Many of us, especially women, have a strong craving to be liked. The reality is that some folks will love you and some will detest you regardless of what you say or do. In fact, if everyone likes you, you're probably playing it too safe. In politics you must accept this, develop a thick skin, and learn not to take criticism – or, for that matter, effusive praise – personally or too seriously. And equally important is the ability to shrug it off quickly so that it doesn't derail your agenda.

During our dual campaigns, we were dismissed by one of Linda's opponents as a "cute novelty act" – never mind that numerous brothers have been elected to Congress. The options were simple: fume or trounce him! Suffice it to say, he is *not* a member of Congress. Similarly, Loretta had a yearlong showdown with a vociferous Bob Dornan, and his venomous tactics ultimately backfired on him – Dornan lost the rematch by a huge margin. Staying focused and thick-skinned is all-important amid such potentially distracting attacks, as it sometimes is when contending with the sexist, patronizing, and dismissive attitudes of certain – in our experience, often male – adversaries and colleagues.

## LORETTA

Our entire family is an effusive, funny, self-deprecating group. We love to make fun of each other – in a nice way – and we're always playing practical jokes. Dad was the original prankster, Mom was quick with the comebacks, and they would laugh along with us when we mimicked their accents or poked fun at what they said. Half the time they didn't even know why they were laughing. All in all, we'd have a good time kidding one another, and although the occasional joke might hit a little too close to home, we learned to laugh at ourselves and roll with the punches.

This, in turn, helped us when we got out into the real world, because we knew not to take things too seriously, as well as to stand up for ourselves when others didn't take *us* too seriously. When I first stepped into the professional world, I frequently had to deal with an attitude of "She's young, how could she know this?" One time, shortly after I had been hired by a particular company, I was in a boardroom with a bunch of people, trying to solve a problem, and the CEO turned to me and asked me to take notes. I said, "Okay, I don't mind doing that, even though you're paying me an awful lot to take notes." He looked at me and asked, "Well, who *are* you?" and I said, "I'm the person who's going to tell you how to solve this problem. That's what you're paying me for." Just being a woman, and being young, I wasn't supposed to be an equal among all these men, so the fact that I was in the boardroom meant I must be a secretary.

In many instances, I felt discounted in the workplace, and this was mostly because I was a woman, not because they had figured out I was a Latina. And the same has applied in Washington. Whatever prejudices I've experienced have usually been due to my gender, and my reaction to them has depended on the circumstances. After all, some people don't even realize they're being dismissive because they do it so much. So, you have to choose your battles and understand the people who are being dismissive. If you're equals and you have a sound rebuttal to someone's derogatory remark, you can challenge that person and say what you think. In other circumstances, it's often best to control your temper and stay silent.

Outside of sports like boxing and wrestling, politics has to be one of the most adversarial professions around, with the participants constantly criticizing and putting one another down. But, I believe that if you develop a reputation for telling the truth and making decisions based upon informed opinions, in the long run voters will trust you. They will also be more willing to forget some of your votes on certain issues because they understand that overall you're not going to be wishy-washy, saying one thing to one group and something else to another group. You just have to be straightforward, and avoid name-calling and saying derogatory things.

When I won the primary during my first congressional campaign, no one even knew who I was. I was not a Democratic Party candidate, but I'd appeared out of nowhere to beat the candidates, and now I was the opponent to Bob Dornan. Well, when he found out who I was, he described me as a dream candidate to run against. "She can't beat me," he told the Orange County newspaper, the *OC Weekly*. "Bob Dornan is a father of five, grandfather of ten, military man, been married forty-one years. She has no kids, no military, no track record. I win."

*Wrong.*

Dismissing me resulted in his defeat. And when we had a rematch two years later, Dornan turned extremely nasty. He went out to the Hispanic community and declared that he was the true Hispanic candidate. He called me a "carpetbagger" even though I was running for election in my hometown, and spread some really malicious rumors.

One year, my Christmas cards carried a photo of my husband, me, and Gretzky, our cat, along with our names. And so, when someone called my campaign office to ask, "What's Wayne Gretzky doing in a picture with the congresswoman and her cat?" it was explained that the cat's name was Gretzky and that the tall, blond, blue-eyed man in the photo was my husband, not the famous ice hockey player. "Her husband?" the caller exclaimed. "I thought her husband was black!" You see, just to stir things up among same of the more conservative white constituents in my district, opponents to my campaign had spread the word that I was married to a black man.

Dornan was willing to go to any lengths to discredit me, and when my only reaction to all the lies, rumors, insinuations, and abuse was to smile, not get riled, and let my work speak for itself, he then resorted to saying I was sly like a fox. The man was unrelenting, but what did I care? I knew the truth. Of course, a lot of times the voter is so uninformed that if something is said enough it sticks to you. But you just have to move forward, hold your head high, and do your work.

The reason people like Bob Dornan do these things is to try to get you off your game. When you run in an election, you need a plan to win, and if it's a great plan and you implement it, then there's a high probability you *will* win. By challenging you, calling you names, placing you in bed with a donkey, or whatever other slurs come to mind, your opponents are trying to divert you from your plan and get you to fight them so that your energy, resources, and focus are misdirected. That's what will make you lose. So, the best thing you can do is ignore them.

That having been said, if you do that too much it can also be perceived as an admission of guilt. These people usually have so much money that they just run ad after ad, and I remember saying, "They're running this ad so much, my husband's really going to think it is true." At some point you think, "When do I have to respond to this?" And I did react once. During the election, I sent a mailer to voters that featured my mom on the front, stating that she'd told her daughter to ignore all the garbage, but that sometimes the garbage just piles up too much and you've got to put your foot down. Her daughter was a lady; the negative campaigning was inappropriate behavior. It was time for it to stop.

It was a response that voters could understand. Everybody in the district—all the mothers and the wives—basically said, "You know what, the mom is right. Enough is enough." The more venomous that Dornan became, the more he turned voters off. We could see the numbers going our way, we could see he was his own worst enemy, and the best thing for me was to behave like a congresswoman. I wanted the votes from these people and I wanted to represent them, but I wasn't about to stoop to this guy's level. In fact, one day I did community office hours in front of a Ralph's supermarket, and I had so ignored Bob Dornan that he actually came and stood in line. Just as I was talking to the woman in front of him and used my arm to move her to one side, he began to scream and yell, alleging I had hit him. People had to intervene.

People see that when I run my campaigns they're extremely positive, and they call to thank me for this, for focusing on what I propose to do, and for not getting in the gutter with my opponents. The problem is, negative politics works, and that's why so many people use it. I combat that by being out in the neighborhood, walking door-to-door, going to community meetings, having office hours so that people can come and see who I am, and ensuring their questions are answered directly by me—"What do you want to know?"

Sometimes there will be people who make stupid comments like "I hear you stir brew on Tuesday nights with a coven of witches," to which I'll reply, "If you believe that, I'm obviously not going to change your mind." Or there will be those who say, "I hear you go over to Planned Parenthood and do the baby-death dance." I mean, how do you respond to these people? I just smile and say, "Thank you very much for showing up today. I'm going to take the next question."

The more you respond with niceness, the nastier some people will get, and that's when everyone else who witnesses this stuff just shakes his or her head and thinks, "The guy's crazy." In most cases, when you're in the public eye, it doesn't do a politician any good to look rattled or thin-skinned. If, say, the agitator really crosses the line and goes after your mother, some people will probably be behind you if you fire back with all guns blazing, but usually it pays to remain calm and let the aggressors hang themselves with their own rope.

Several years ago I was on the House floor, talking to Charlie Rangel, a very important Democrat who's now the Ways and Means Committee chairman, and I said, "Gosh, Charlie, these days I can't pick my nose in public or have toilet paper stuck in my nylons. I just feel like I can't move or see or do anything because everybody knows who I am, and that weighs on me. It's a heavy burden."

"Loretta, it is not a burden," Charlie replied. "It is a responsibility and it is a privilege to serve in this chamber, and those people who elect you expect the best out of you every single day. And the best means you're not going to pick your nose, you're not going to have toilet paper stuck in your nylons, and you're going to have your makeup on and your hair combed nicely. Because the day you believe that it's too much of a responsibility to stay on the even road and avoid doing negative things is the day you should consider leaving this chamber."

And you know what? He was right. I choose to represent the people, and they have a right to expect the best out of me. I'm not always at my best — some days are much better than others — but I never complain anymore about having to fly, not getting enough sleep, turning up too late to vote, or being unable to drink my coffee without somebody approaching me. If people want to speak to me it's because they need something solved, they wish to express themselves, they don't think that government listens to them, and they want answers, and that's all part of the job.

Not that unwelcome intrusion should be part of the job. It's one thing placing myself in the public eye and in the firing line of political opponents, but when I was sitting down recently and spotted a paparazzo crouching across the way, aiming a long telephoto lens straight up my skirt, that was a bit much. I went over to him and said, "What the hell are you doing?" Those guys overstep the mark, and I had no problem telling him exactly what I thought.

On the other hand, when Joe Baca made his remark about me, my decision to quit the Hispanic caucus had nothing to do with being thin-skinned. He has a history in Sacramento as an elected official, he has a history in Washington, D.C., as an elected official. I have my own eleven-year history as an elected official, and I didn't have to belong to a group that would retain him as chairman when he was going to be disrespectful in that way. That was my choice, and people could think whatever they wanted. They could believe his "I didn't say that," or they could believe my "Oh yes he did." They know what type of person he is and they know what type of person I am. So, I'm very comfortable with how that played out.

His comment was made to discredit me after I had endorsed someone who was running against his son. Well, that's his problem. When you say those types of things in public—and it was in public, because there were numerous people in the room—that reflects on *him*, not me. And considering how the media reacted, as well as the way people in Washington and around the nation reacted—all of the e-mails I received from Latinas and those who knew this guy, saying, "You go, girl. Stand up for your rights. It was the typical reaction of a man who's been cornered"—there was no need for me to open my mouth. Why should I? People know who I am, and they came to my defense.

Many political people read the blogs every day, but if I did that I'd probably think I'm a terrible person. The fact of the matter is, there's plenty of derogatory stuff on the outside because you make enemies over time. Some of them haven't even met you, but they perceive you in a certain way—If you're a Latina woman in politics in California, you must be a liberal; and if your last name is Sánchez, you must be an illegal immigrant. So much of it is crazy. Those people don't check the facts, they don't care about the facts, they've got their own facts, and some of them unfortunately are the biggest bloggers. They have nothing better to do with their time.

Within the Congress are there still colleagues who dismiss me? Yes, there are—people who don't sit on the committees, people who don't see my work on a day-to-day basis, people who don't hear my questions. I appeared on a TV program, talking about habeus corpus and military commissions and what's going on with the alleged terrorists we're holding at Guantánamo. I spent an hour referring to the history, the Constitution, what the Supreme Court has done, what the president has done, what's wrong, how we need to address the problems of holding these people in custody. Afterward I walked into the chamber and a longtime Congress member who's never been on my committee said, "Man, you really knew what you were talking about on that TV show!"

Just by the way he said this I could tell he was thinking, *"I never realized you had a brain!"*

I just thanked him and smiled. That's what you have to do a lot of the time, although there are also occasions when you really have to stand up for yourself on the House floor.

After I beat Bob Dornan by just 984 votes in my first congressional campaign, he contested the result, alleging voter fraud, and there was a congressional investigation. During that period, I was in the House, but I wasn't a full member, and night after night there were votes to try to get rid of me. One night, Tom Campbell, a Republican out of San Jose, gave a speech in which he quoted statistics that purportedly illustrated why I shouldn't be in the Congress. This guy had been a law professor at Stanford University, but I was sure his statistics were wrong. So after he finished I went down to the House floor and defended myself.

Vern Ehlers, a Republican out of Michigan, was chairman of the task force that was investigating the voter fraud allegations and trying to decide whether or not I should be in the Congress. After I finished responding to Campbell, Ehlers took the floor and spouted a load of gobbledegook about how I was out of line and they were only trying to be fair. I just shook my head and started to walk out of the chamber, at which point Vern ran up to me and said, "Loretta, I just want you to know this is not personal."

I turned on my heels, went face-to-face with him, and replied, "You better believe this is personal, Vern."

Vern prided himself on being even-keeled and fair and bipartisan, but I shook my finger in his face and said, "Statistically speaking, you know I'm right, and this is just a lot of garbage from your party. Everything in Orange County is controlled by the Republican Party, so there's no place where I could have cheated in this election, but you guys are being political and I've just had it with you! When you say it's not personal, it *is* personal, because you're making my life miserable every single day the more you uphold what Dornan is doing."

Vern's face was turning red and his voice was rising against mine, but I just told him to forget it. You know, "Don't even try to tell me you're the wise man attempting to be impartial here. This is just a pile of nonsense."

He was clearly shocked that I would turn around, stand up for myself, and basically tell him off, not least since he was the task force chairman. Alcee Hastings, an African American colleague of mine from Florida, saw this happening as he was walking out of the chamber, and he got between us and pulled us apart. He took me aside and said, "Loretta, let it go. Just let it go."

I'd absolutely had enough of Mr. Vern Ehlers telling

me he was going to be judicious and he was going to be fair. Maybe he was trying to convince himself, but he wasn't going to convince *me*. The reality was, he was being pushed by the Republican leadership, and he could have admitted that. All he had to say was, "I know what the statistics are, Loretta, and you just have to understand this is politics." I'd have far more respect for someone who would tell me that than someone who's trying to persuade me that he's fair and impartial when we both know darn well that isn't the case.

Vern avoided me for a long time after that little episode. And although we now say hi to one another, we've never had a working kinship, because he was wrong and I think he knew he was wrong. Then again, I also had a failing in that whole scenario. I was too naïve and too new to the Congress to understand that the Republican leadership was really pushing him, and that he either had to follow orders or he would have lost the chairmanship. Had I known that, I probably would have said, "You know, Vern, you're an okay guy. It's just too bad that you're a puppet for the Republicans." Instead, he got the full barrage, and people very rarely get that from me.

## LINDA

Having learned to stand up for myself in the face of my brothers' teasing, I knew how to spar verbally from an early age. Our parents didn't have a lot of tolerance for us crying to them about arguments between the siblings—their attitude was "Work it out among yourselves"—and so at home and within the family I was accustomed to fending for myself. However, in the larger world that wasn't always the case, especially in situations where there wasn't equal power.

For example, when I first started my career, if I had a boss who was verbally abusive or unfairly critical of me, I wouldn't want to get into a verbal altercation with him and risk losing my job. It took me years to learn the right balance. I particularly remember having a confrontation with the boss at the law firm where I worked and challenging him on something. In my heart I knew I was right, so I spoke up. But there were negative consequences from that. Some of my plum assignments were pulled away from me, and while I wasn't too brokenhearted because I'd just received a clear signal that it was probably time to move on, I also learned from that.

Sometimes, you have to estimate whether it's worth accepting a criticism and keeping your mouth shut, or whether you should speak up because you think it's unwarranted. There are times when you have to accept the criticism whether it's fair or unfair, and just shake it off, not stew over it, and focus on what needs to get done. Certainly, campaigning is very much like that. Loretta told me, "Linda, you tend to take things very personally, and if you take all of the unkind and mean things said about you to heart, you won't last through the campaign. You have to learn to let a lot of it roll off your back."

That's what I did. Part of the warfare when you're campaigning is psychological. Opponents say terrible things about you, most of them not true, or they may be 10 percent true and 90 percent skewed. You try to respond to some of the criticism because you don't want to let your detractors think you're not going to challenge them. However, you've really got to be selective in terms of what you choose to respond to and what you decide to ignore. Some issues are substantial, and others are more like little dogs yapping at your heels.

A common assertion was that I was too young and inexperienced to run for office. Some of my opponents said that, and I absolutely had to respond because experience is a prime factor when people are deciding whom to vote for. So, I pointed out that, while I may not have held elected office, I'd been involved with local issues as a community activist. Then there were the allegations that I had three different addresses, one of which was a PO box. I didn't think that would top people's list when they were trying to determine which candidate would best represent their viewpoint, so I responded but I didn't dwell on it. I explained that one address was where my campaign was physically located, one was the campaign PO box, and one was the address to the home I bought prior to the census and redistricting.

Ultimately, although my opponents tried to make a lot of it, it really wasn't a big issue in the campaign.

It's a sad fact of life that negative campaigning is effective, otherwise candidates wouldn't do it. Yes, everybody wants positive, issue-based campaigning, but the polls illustrate that a lot of people don't vote on the issues, they vote on the personalities. Part of the problem is that, unlike some other countries, we don't have publicly funded campaigns where all of the candidates get equal time on TV. In America, whoever raises the most money has the best chance to put his or her message across, and you often have to do it in thirty-second sound bites. So, you don't have time to explain a complex issue, how you voted on it, or how you liked some but not all of the bill and still felt you had to vote for it. Instead, people resort to attack ads.

Still, there also comes a tipping point where, if everything you're doing is negative, there's a backlash. When I ran, I ran against people who had voting records, and I don't think there's anything wrong with highlighting those records so long as the votes are indicative of their priorities and you are factual in terms of what you're saying about them. When you are campaigning, it's legitimate to draw distinctions between you and another candidate, whereas personal attacks, in my opinion, are not okay. Taking something that has a kernel of truth and blowing it out of proportion so that it bears no resemblance to the truth is unacceptable.

Dealing with opponents is one thing, but when I first hit the campaign trail it was especially tough getting used to rejection from members of the public. Once the election was over I had a whole newfound empathy for people who ask others out on dates and get turned down—it must be a very similar experience. When you sell a product door-to-door, whether it's insurance, encyclopedias, or candy, if people say no to you, you always have a small safety valve, rationalizing that "they're not rejecting me, they just don't need or like the product." But when you're a candidate and you're selling yourself, if people say no or are rude to you (or, yes, even slam the door in your face), they're rejecting you. It's very personal, and that's very hard to take.

Still, you have to take the good with the bad. People don't slam the door in your face very often. That might happen at one out of seventy-five houses, and at ten of them there might be a very positive response to your ideas, so you have to dwell on the motivating factors more than the failures. Otherwise, you may as well pack up and go home. Dwelling on failure will paralyze you, so if people are rude or completely disinterested, you have to play a psychological game with yourself and make excuses for their behavior— "Well, maybe she can't talk right now because a sick relative's on the phone." Anything to avoid feeling totally discouraged, even if, overwhelmingly, most people are surprised—and very interested—when a congresswoman shows up on their doorstep to talk to them and ask for their support.

A quick temper is never a good thing in politics. It can be very detrimental, because when you're angry you don't always think clearly, and if you speak rashly that will usually come back to haunt you. Plus, your opponents will know what buttons to push. My brothers are masters at knowing what buttons to push, and over time I learned they were doing this to provoke a reaction. Now, when they bait me about certain things, I just appear nonplussed and don't say much, and that gets them to stop.

The same applies to the press. If you respond to their allegations, it piques their interest—"Why is she reacting so vehemently?" There are so many inaccuracies in what is reported, you just learn to roll with it. And besides, no one else's perspective will entirely match your own. However, whereas celebrities sometimes choose to largely ignore negative articles and reviews, as a policy maker I think it's always important to read what the press has to write.

There's a saying in Washington, "Don't believe your own press," because your press is, of course, designed to paint you in the best light, and it will be to your detriment if you start to believe that everything you do is perfect. Your ego will expand and you may become dismissive of other's ideas because you think yours are best. So, you really have to stay grounded. After all, an overly friendly press can be just as damaging as a harsh, critical press, and journalists—like most people—love to build you up so that later they can tear you down. That's why, if you're experiencing effusive press coverage, you should also look out for the sharp stick that, at some point, will be poking you in the eye. And, while it's important to read what is written about you, it's equally important to take it with a grain of salt.

Today's story is often in tomorrow's wastebasket, but beware of the one that leaves you with a bad reputation that sticks. Here in Washington, there's an obsession with having the most up-to-date information, and so when the press knocks you and writes an unfavorable piece, it will often make tomorrow's—or even today's—news. Where you really get into trouble is if it's widely syndicated or repeated in other articles. That's when you should start to worry.

The same sometimes happens when you have an off day and either speak in anger or put your foot in your mouth. The embarrassment may last only a day or two, but there's always the potential that three years down the line it could be revived by an opponent and splashed across the front page of a campaign mailer. The spoken and the written word both have a lot of power when you are in public office, and so you have to be careful, but you also have to realize that you can't control what people are going to say or write about you.

When politicians or the press are spewing bile about you, to a certain extent they're counting on people not knowing the full story. And again, you have to determine whether it's worthwhile responding, because sometimes, instead of nipping it in the bud, your response can turn a one-day story into a three- or four-day story. If you choose to respond, you must figure out the proper response. Overdoing it will prompt people to wonder why you care so much—"There must be more to it"—while a weak, perfunctory reply will lead them to suspect you really don't have a good defense.

When I first got elected, Bill O'Reilly invited Loretta and me to appear on his Fox News TV show to talk about being the first ever sisters in Congress. During a preinterview the day before, we discussed our background and what all this meant to us. But then, once we were on the show, O'Reilly was interested only in grilling us on immigration while spewing venom about how illegal immigrants are the source of all ills in this country. Since our position on immigration was different from his, he was attacking us like we were part of the problem, and it quickly became clear that we had been ambushed. He was trying to catch us off guard to make us look stupid, and at a certain point I told him he's a panic merchant who pedals in fear.

We were in a different studio than Bill O'Reilly was, so we appeared via satellite, and we were subjected to "stepping on the mic," which means your microphone's volume is turned down. That's what was done to me as soon as I uttered the words *panic merchant*, but the point had been made. When dealing with the media, I can often expose or underscore someone's agenda by way of a quick comeback stated in a unique or funny manner. But at the same time, I also refuse to go on shows where you're shouting at each other and whoever gets heard is the person who shouts the loudest. That's not my style.

When you're in the public eye, you constantly have to evaluate what to say and what not to say, and sometimes I feel like I'm doing a balancing act...quite literally. One night during my first term, I was in heels and a skirt, and there were these high steps in the chamber which I really couldn't step down. There was a two-foot drop, and because I was young and athletic I'd normally jump down instead of using the other, more shallow steps. However, on this night, when I jumped off the top step in my high heels, I slipped and I fell, hurting my back. The sharp pain made me feel nauseous, but some people helped me to my feet and they took me up to the speaker's balcony so that I might catch my breath. Well, the next day there was a report that I had been drunk on the floor of Congress.

It was ridiculous, not least because I had returned for the last vote of the evening. My colleagues had wanted to take me to the physician, but the pain had subsided and the vote was an important one, so I'd gone back to the chamber, and now here was this story in one of the scandal sheets on the Hill, accusing me of passing out on the floor. I mean, there were enough people there who could definitely vouch for the fact that didn't happen, and that's what I said when the press sought comment, but what else could I do? We didn't want to blow it up into more of a story than it really was, so we just issued a statement and then had to let it go. There was no way to disprove what didn't happen. However, it may have been this supposedly "drunken" incident which then fed another nonstory several years later.

I do stand-up comedy in Washington, and I compete in a contest which benefits Bread for the City, a charity that helps feed the homeless. In 2006, when I actually won the contest, I had a routine that poked fun at my blue-collar roots—although I come from California, which is a wonderful wine-producing state, I don't really drink wine. I prefer beer, and so I did this piece about Miller High Life, which my dad still drinks to this day. It isn't a fancy microbrew, it's a very blue-collar beer—"The Champagne of Bottled Beer"—and I love it, because to me there's nothing more refreshing on a hot day than a cold Miller High Life.

Anyway, I was doing this routine at the Improv comedy club, I had a beer in my hand as a prop, and every now and then I would take a sip to emphasize a punch line and give people time to take it in and laugh. Well, some disgruntled blogger in my district saw my act when it was later broadcast on C-SPAN, and he took photos, posted one on his blog site of me with a beer in my hand just as I was about to blink, and wrote this whole piece about how I was drunk onstage and needed to go to rehab—an absurd allegation on so many levels! If I had been drunk doing stand-up comedy, everyone in the world would have known about it, and I wouldn't have been able to win the contest, because when you're that drunk you can't function. But, here was this venomous blog about my being a party girl in Washington with a major drinking problem.

What to do? Responding to this might just lend credence to the craziness. I figured that very few people would visit his blog site and read what he'd written, and even fewer would believe it in light of the hard work that I do within the district. So, I kept quiet. Some friendly Democrats called to ask if I'd seen what was on this blog site, and I told them, "Yes, it's completely fabricated and I'm not even going to respond. Doing that would only engage this person in dialogue, and I have other things to do with my time."

This in no way means I can't take criticism. When constituents criticize me for my vote on an issue or my stance on an issue, their criticisms are sometimes warranted. I look at the issue from their perspective, think about it, and conclude that their remarks are valid. There's nothing wrong with that. No one's infallible. For example, Lynwood, one of the cities that I represent, was going through a lot of political turmoil, and I supported some of the members of the city council who had come to me, seeking my endorsement. In response to allegations of corruption, they had signed an "honest government" pledge, and so I did end up endorsing them. Months later, after that election, a movement arose to recall these people from office, and I was criticized by some city residents for not opposing the recall and by other residents for not endorsing the recall.

The consensus of opinion appeared to be "Let the people of Lynwood figure out who they want to represent them," and at the end of the day I thought that was valid. Let the election take place and let the residents decide whom they want on their city council. Don't get involved in that process. So, that's what I did. I stayed out of things and let the election go forward. That was very hard, because I wanted to see good government at the city level and I wanted to see competent people with whom I could work. However, public criticism persuaded me to let the voters decide. And although that may have required restraint on my part, it certainly didn't anger or upset me.

Personal put-downs are another matter. Sexist, patronizing, and dismissive attitudes are a sad fact of life for women on the Hill, and we really have to develop a thick skin to deal with the people who have those attitudes. Congress is unique in that, if a colleague behaves in a discriminatory or unfair manner, we don't really have a company-type boss to whom we can complain. The constituents who elect us are our bosses, and so unless we're prepared to visit their district and whine, "This guy's condescending and disrespectful toward women," there's nothing we can do.

Therefore, we have to learn to work with people who are often like that or find ways to work around them. Without a doubt, there are certain members of Congress who still believe women don't belong there, and there are those who see women just as sexual objects. I've had members proposition me, and there are even ones twice my age who have this sort of rock-star mentality that everybody wants to be their groupie. When they are turned down politely but firmly, some of them still won't take no for an answer. Soon, the word gets around: they are the ones to avoid, the ones who are always a little too friendly or a little too touchy-feely.

Having sought the help of other members when I first got elected, I tried to make time during my second term to go and chat with the new female members and give them some of my insights. I'd only been in Congress for two years, but I still wanted to pass on some of the wisdom that I had collected during my first term, and part of the discussion concerned the attitudes of certain male members and how to deal with them or, if necessary, try to work around them. Some of the women found this really helpful.

Politics, for me, is largely about camaraderie and teamwork, and since I love playing baseball and talking about it over a drink, I don't mind being treated like one of the guys. I enjoy being humorous with my colleagues, and although my jokes aren't always clean, there's never any intent other than humor behind them. That having been said, among all the women in Congress there probably are one or two who try to use their femininity or their good looks to finagle things out of people, and the other members really resent that. This is a job, and all of us should respect our colleagues and what they do.

Sometimes the bad attitudes belong to outsiders. There will be witnesses who come before our committees for hearings and not only look at me like, "Oh, what does she know?" but are also rude to me when I ask them questions. Well, I'm a former litigator, so if they underestimate me they do so at their peril, because I'll just fillet anyone who's condescending. I remember one hearing where I asked a witness a very simple yes or no question, and he embarked on this convoluted answer knowing full well that each of us only had five minutes for questioning. Finally, I said, "Excuse me, you still haven't answered my question," and one of the other members of the committee said, "Mr. Chairman, I would ask that Miss Sánchez not interrupt the witness when the witness is trying to give his answer."

This was when the Democrats were in the minority, and the chairman turned to me and said, "Miss Sánchez, you have to give the witness a chance to answer." Without even missing a beat I replied, "With all due respect, Mister Chairman, this is my five minutes to question. I've asked for a very simple yes or no answer and I haven't gotten one. I'd like to get answers to the questions that I have, and I would appreciate it if the chairman wouldn't interrupt *me* during my time."

He was really taken aback, but did he honestly think I was going to just roll over and let this witness run out the clock with some BS answer? I had no choice but to be assertive. Then again, in 2005, when we had the hearing on steroids in baseball, Curt Schilling of the Boston Red Sox also had the most disdainful attutude. I quoted some facts before asking a question, and when I asked him to respond he said in a sneering tone, "The question is?" I said, "The question is, have you ever made the problem of use among players that you have heard rumors of—made that known to somebody responsible?" I didn't back down. He was really arrogant and obviously thought he was being clever, so I just went back at him.

I've seen witnesses be very respectful to the chairman, as well as to other more senior male members, but as soon as the questions are being asked by those of us who are younger, female, or both, then they don't feel obligated to answer. The ex-Attorney General, Alberto Gonzales, was a prime example. He was evasive and apparently felt he didn't need to cooperate. Well, he did. Our job is to provide oversight, and on a couple of occasions I really stuck it to him because he had this curious attitude that he shouldn't have to stoop to answer the questions of the Judiciary Committee in general and of me in particular.

My background as a litigator was really good training for dealing with all this. When you try cases, you know how to structure your questions in order to get the testimony out of a witness that will help prove your point, and that's one of the biggest skills that I employ in Congress. Thanks to my legal background, I know how to question witnesses, and so anyone who thinks they can sidestep the issues and give me the brush-off had better watch out.

# 9

# Full Circle

Among the better known statements of César Chávez is "We cannot seek achievement for ourselves and forget about progress and prosperity for our community…Our ambitions must be broad enough to include the aspirations and needs of others, for their sakes and our own." Not surprisingly, this concept was etched on our psyches during our early years. It's hard to imagine a Hispanic family that doesn't emphasize the linked values of family and community.

Still, sharing the wealth concerns much more than financial affluence. All of us who enjoy any measure of success owe it to others to help them along the same path, and this points to not only our own experiences – raising scholarship money for poor students, fighting for medical and educational rights for the children of immigrants – but also the life of she who taught us, our mother, Maria Macias. We have spent our lives watching her "pay it forward," even before she had much to give, and we only hope that we can have the kind of impact she has had on countless others.

## LORETTA

From the time her father died, our mom was forced to give up what she really wanted, which was an education and a career, in order to take care of her brothers and sisters. That set a lifelong pattern of giving of herself, and when she married our father and had seven children, she then had to invest the time to really build that family and inspire her children to not only do well for themselves but also participate within the community for the greater good.

There are so many examples of how she learned the ropes in a foreign land and contributed to what, for her, was basically a new world. She was the Brownie leader, the fund-raiser for schools, the room mother. She used every talent she had to ensure that her children were included in the community, and even when her children were too old for many of those activities and developed into their own people, Mom was still involving herself in the community, going back to school, becoming a teacher, helping her students and their families, participating on political action committees, raising money for them, getting to know politicians, and pushing issues at those politicians.

I always used to laugh because, during the four years that I was a congresswoman when President Clinton was in the White House, Mom met him maybe four or five times at fund-raisers and when he campaigned for me, and she'd never miss an opportunity to take him to task on an issue that she believed he wasn't paying enough attention to or had sold out on. It was so embarrassing. She'd be in a receiving line and he'd know it was my mom—he loved our family and knew us all, because that's the way he is—and so she would hug him and then she'd start in with, "I don't understand why you did this! You have to correct it!"

This was in front of everybody, and even if people were supposed to have two minutes in the receiving line, she would take twenty minutes to outline the issue and explain what the president, with his power, could do to change it. I'd be cringing, and it just became a topic of laughter in our family—"What's Mom going to tell him this time?"

When she was raising seven kids, we were often barely making ends meet, but we managed. Dad was always employed. Even when he lost his job, he would go out the very next day and find a new one, because he had the responsibility of feeding nine mouths. At those times, it was really just about holding on to the roof over our heads and putting food on the table, yet if Mom saw kids in the neighborhood who didn't have a jacket—kids who were much poorer than ourselves—she would go door-to-door, sell tamales, and raise the money to ensure those kids had galoshes when it was raining and jackets when it was cold. We were one of the poorest families in the area of Anaheim where we grew up, yet Mom always thought we had so much more than everybody else and that they had far larger needs than we did. So, she would do something about it, without prompting from anyone else.

Helping others is undoubtedly characteristic of the Hispanic community. I represent some very poor Hispanic families in places like Santa Ana, and if one of them, for example, doesn't have the money to bury someone who's just died, the neighborhood will pull together and maybe donate or collect recyclable bottles to raise the $300, $400, or $500 that it'll cost to buy a pinewood box, secure a plot, and lay to rest somebody's child or somebody's father. In that sense, the Hispanic community is a very collective "we." And even if, as has been said about American culture, it's changed in recent times to more of a "me me me" society, then it has done so to a much smaller extent. Hispanic culture is still about the collective "we," yet our mother went above and beyond that, and her example had a major impact on *all* of her children's lives.

My brother Iggy—Ignacio Jr.—graduated from Cal State Fullerton, and he and our brother Michael own an equipment leasing company in my district. It's one of the most successful and fastest-growing companies in the area, and Iggy is very involved in raising scholarship money for students who go to Cal State Fullerton, which is considered to be a "Hispanic-serving Institution," a nonprofit institution that has at least 25 percent full-time Hispanic students in its student body. In other words, even at the national level it's a university that is recognized for being able to attract, retain, and graduate Hispanic students. Percentage wise, far fewer Hispanics than Caucasians acquire bachelor degrees and since elementary schools are experiencing a huge influx of Hispanic children, from a workforce perspective this is a negative for America. We need to be training these people. They are very underrepresented at the college level, and so Iggy is moving mountains to really help in that arena.

For his part, Michael is the primary caretaker for our father, who has Alzheimer's. When we discovered that Dad had the disease, Michael was the one who figured out what this meant, what we had to do, and what we might expect to happen. He served as the path for our family to know how to accept and deal with the situation as constructively and positively as possible. He went to the Alzheimer's Association in Orange County, within a year he was sitting on the board, and now he chairs its big annual fund-raiser. So, it wasn't just a case of his finding information to help his family deal with this problem—"I'll go and I'll take." Instead, it was "I'll go and I'll not only take, but I'll also create and give."

Our other sister, Martha, is an investment broker for Morgan Stanley. She's very busy, she's very successful, and she has two young daughters, yet she somehow also finds the time to serve as president of their school's PTA and involve herself in other community activities. Then there's our eldest brother, Henry, who's in the mortgage banking industry as well being as an artist. When he started selling some of his artwork, he immediately set his mind to raising money for artists with potential who haven't been successful yet. And finally there's Frank, a former marine who served his country and now is a civil engineer with the city of Long Beach, who's involved at various levels with professional organizations that raise money for the sciences.

Linda and I weren't the only ones in our family to

take a leaf from our mother's book. Helping others was ingrained in us from an early age. Whether or not I wanted to, I was filling out immigration forms for my mother's students and their families, and when Mom ran the fireworks stand for the local Boy Scout troop she would call and say, "I need you to help sell fireworks on Saturday," and there we were. If she said, "I need you to come to my classroom and talk to the kids about being educated," we were there, too. When she said, "Come," we went and did.

When we were young, Mom brought us in to work on things, and we continued in that vein, looking for what we could help with out there in our spare time. On my own, once I had an MBA and I was working, I became the president of the National Society of Hispanic MBAs in Los Angeles, and then I started programs at the local junior high and high schools to raise money for scholarships, to add summer classes, and to do math and science.

## LINDA

One of my favorite things to do is talk to groups of young people in high school and college, because many of them are at a time in their lives when they're unsure where they are heading. I always tell them, "You're going to get where you want to go if you stay focused on your goal. But when you get there and you have that breathing space, you have an obligation to help somebody who is either struggling or is unsure and needs advice. Because it's only by building on the success of others that we progress."

Some time back, I spoke at a college where a mother told me that her daughter had graduated but failed to get into the law school she wanted to attend. "Since you were an attorney," she said, "could you sit down with her for fifteen minutes and talk to her about your experience of applying to law school? Maybe you can help her see that, even if she doesn't get into the one school that she wants, there are other options available." I told her, "Absolutely I'm willing to do that. Call my scheduler and we'll set up a time."

There are tons of things that matter in young people's lives, and I could make a million excuses, saying I'm too busy doing this or doing that, and that this girl needs to figure out what she wants to do, but I had people who stopped along the way to help me. There was my sixth grade teacher, Mr. Gardener, who encouraged me to be an attorney. He saw me always sticking up for the underdog and defending the unpopular position in class debates, and he said, "You've got the makings of an attorney." Well, somewhere that stuck in my head, because later, when I was trying to figure out what I wanted to do, I heard his voice telling me that, and I subsequently pursued a law career.

I always had wonderful mentors. When I played softball as a high school senior, a friend on the team was a fabulous athlete but she wasn't doing well in her classes. So, I asked her if there was a teacher that she liked who might be able to help, and she couldn't name *one*. She couldn't name one throughout her entire academic career, and I thought that was really sad because I could pick at least half a dozen teachers who had really influenced me and helped me and encouraged me and inspired me. Sometimes, it just takes that one person encouraging or inspiring you for you to believe that you can pursue or achieve a specific dream.

In the workplace, I've also had mentors, and so when some people claim that all their success is of their own doing, I don't believe that. Somewhere, somebody has helped them. It was instilled in me by my parents that you owe a debt to society to try to leave it a little better than how it was handed to you, to try to make that path a little bit easier for the next person. If people just credited their accomplishments to themselves and didn't share information, we wouldn't progress as a society. I mean, the scientific breakthroughs that we've had are based on the breakthoughs that other people have had and shared.

We can give back to the community in so many ways: inspirational or motivational help, college scholarships, financial assistance for people who are in trouble. I regard all of these things as an obligation in the most positive way, and one that

I'm more than happy to try to fulfill at all levels. I mean, it starts with individual casework in our office and it goes on to broad policy decisions that impact millions of people.

For example, we had a case in our office of a veteran who had been appealing his disability assessment. He had been assessed at something like a 20 percent disability, and he kept fighting it because he knew he was more disabled and should be receiving more compensation. This had been going on for six or seven years, and by the time he came to our office he was quite literally going to be evicted from his apartment because he couldn't afford the payments. Well, we were able to get him reassessed, it was determined that his disability was much worse than had previously been diagnosed, and he was paid $86,000 in back benefits that he had been entitled to and never received.

Talk about making a difference in one person's life! One minute he was a step away from being homeless, and the next he was able to stay and support himself. Imagine what that must have felt like, not to mention the vindication after all those years of struggle and fighting for what was rightfully his. It turned out that he had been right all along. When you're able to do that for somebody, it's an incredibly good feeling. It's like getting paid in something that's more valuable than money. And it's not just about alleviating poverty or financial pressure, it's also about providing people with the freedom to realize their own potential.

## LORETTA

I have a Republican colleague from Texas, and during a debate with him on the radio several years ago he said, "Poor people are poor because they want to be." If I've become more partisan over time, it's because Republicans make statements like that. Not *all* Republicans, just some, and I often ask myself, "Are they living in the real world?" How could they even say a thing like that? I'd love to ask them, "So, do you really think that if a first grade teacher asks the children what they want to be when they grow up, amid answers like 'I want to be a police officer,' 'I want to be a fireman,' 'I want to be a teacher,' and 'I want to be a nurse,' one kid will stand up and say, 'I want to be poor'?"

Since I've been in office I've had more of an opportunity to hear dumb rhetoric—from *both sides*—and when people ask me, "How do we know who to believe? How do we know who to vote for? How do we get the information?" my answer's always the same: "How much time do you want to spend on this? If you only want to spend a little time, then you'll only have basic information and you'll do what I used to do when I voted—'Do I know this guy? Have I heard his name before? Has he been in a scandal? I don't know any of these people, so is there a woman on the ballot? Is there a Hispanic on the ballot?'"

That's how a lot of people vote. They have real lives going on. They don't have time to sit around and read the newspapers and watch the debates and meet the candidates. But if they're concerned about education, and if they do hear what the candidates have to say, this will probably include both the Democrat and the Republican saying things like, "I'm for education. We need educated kids! We need to keep them off the street!" Well, yeah. But still it comes down to whom they should believe. Is one better than the other? Discerning all the differences takes a lot of time. And so, again, how much time do you want to spend?

Most voters are uninformed, and I understand why. However, it doesn't make for having the best possible government, and as I tell seniors in high school when they're about to reach the voting age, "Your government is only as good as the time you put into it. If you participate, the government will be better. If you don't participate, a few people who spend a lot of time participating in that government will be running everything."

If I hadn't gone into politics, but had tried to build a family and was involved in raising money for the Boy Scouts, I would still be a good community player. But I'm also not sure I'd sit down at the computer for an hour every day, trying to figure out the difference between all the politicians in my area. That having been said, I'd like to think I would have still become a Democrat. After all, I hope I would have been bright enough, what with all the bad Bush stuff, to tell myself, "Wow, I've got to get rid of that label *fast!*" I have seen that happen many times over the last few years, with Republicans in Orange County saying, "I'm an independent. I've changed my registration to 'decline to state.'" It takes something really bad for that to happen, but watch out, it's on the rise across the nation.

## LINDA

When I was in my mid-twenties, I went out with friends for somebody's birthday celebration and I began talking politics with this guy who said he'd never voted in his life. I said, "Never?" and he replied, "Well, okay, I voted once."

I was intrigued. "What did you vote on?" I asked, and he said, "Several years ago, California had an initiative on the ballot to increase the tax on cigarettes."

"Don't tell me," I interjected, "you're a smoker."

"That's right," he replied, "so I voted against it. However, it didn't matter, because it lost anyway."

I said, "Okay, so let me get this straight. You registered to vote and you voted only because you didn't want to pay more for your cigarettes."

"Exactly," he said. "They already cost enough."

"But do you realize that the economic impact of all the other elections in which you didn't vote was ten billion times greater than that one cigarette pack?"

"What do you mean?"

"The people who you vote for—or don't vote for—are the ones who decide how the money gets spent. They're the ones who decided whether or not college will be affordable for you, whether or not the roads in front of your house will get fixed, whether or not there will be job retraining programs if you become unemployed, and whether or not you're going to have affordable health care. We elect people to make those decisions for us, and if you're not participating in that, then the ones who make those decisions could be voting against your interests. Just think about the economic impact that will have on your life. A hell of a lot more than one measly cigarette pack."

I don't know if I convinced him, but it's true. After all that certain people went through in this country to earn the right to vote, it defies belief that there's only a 30 percent turnout when we go to the polls. If you are disengaged, don't complain about what you get. You've surrendered your right to complain if you're not voting. The reason I got into politics is that I didn't believe the choices of candidates I had available to me were the choices I wanted. And I could either sit and complain about it or I could do something about it. So, I decided to run for office, because in my heart of hearts I felt

I could do a better job. And I try every day to do that job to the best of my ability.

Most people don't have to run for office. They just have to pay attention to what their elected representatives are doing, and they just have to show up and vote. They shouldn't be passive and accept what is handed to them. They should be proactive and shape their own destiny. And they should also be kind to others. That may sound trite, but it can get repaid in a million different ways. You never know when it will come back to you—or it may *never* come back to you—but there should be enough joy in the doing to do it anyway.

One time, when I was a struggling college student, I was at a fast-food drive-through, picking up something to eat, and when I pulled up to the cashier's window I was informed that the person in front of me had paid my check. He didn't know my situation, he just did something kind, and because of that I've done the same for others, picking up people's tabs at the dry cleaners. These are little things, and again, you may not know who you're helping or what their circumstances are, but there's a certain joy in just being kind to people or helping them in small ways that can really make an impact.

## LORETTA

In Congress, there are lots of ways for a member to bring people together to help nonprofit organizations that are doing a good job in the community. We can sit down and talk to them—"What is it that you're doing? This is a good program, how do we get national funding for it?" Some of it comes out of the federal budget, some of it comes out of foundations, and some of it comes out of making personal and campaign contributions. Congresspeople can go to their meetings, address their volunteers, and motivate them to continue with those types of things.

All of it has to do with putting earmarks in the federal budget for some of these programs. Donna Shalala and I kept pressuring President Clinton in 2000—his last year in office—to put a billion extra dollars into Head Start, and his people kept taking it out of the budget, and we kept pushing to put it back in. Well, the result was, and continues to be, those billion extra dollars at the funding level to help more students get into the program, and I'm very proud of that. I think it has a significant impact on children across the nation.

There are funds in the federal budget for such things as the Migrant Education Program, the TRIO Programs, and the CAMP Program. These are programs that identify immigrant children, assist them with going to university, and provide money to the universities to do outreach and retain those students. Because if you come from a family where no one's gone to university, and you go to a university and see two Hispanics among ten thousand students, there's a strong temptation to drop out. It's not your peer group; it's a difficult change. Who do you turn to if you're having problems, and will you get homesick? All these types of things could apply to an eighteen- or nineteen- or twenty-year-old who's experiencing something new, and we've put money in the budgets for these universities to have counselors and to have programs that encourage and help and retain these students.

## LINDA

There really is a huge dropout rate among Hispanic students, and some of this is because of economic pressure from the family. Sometimes, just showing an interest in somebody or caring about somebody is all that person needs. And while kids must be made aware of how important their education is, in many cases so must the parents. Unlike our mom and dad, there are many struggling parents who, as soon as their kids can work, value extra income over higher education that might lead to a great career.

I speak to groups of parents, and I explain that my mom didn't just tell us education was important and she didn't just say we had to study. Kids hate parents who are "do as I say, not as I do." Instead, Mom went back to school and *showed* us that education was important. She sat at the dinner table and did her homework while we did ours. We followed her example, not just her words, and our parents were interested and involved in whatever we did. That makes such a difference, and so do the volunteer programs that reach out to the community and require only small investments of yourself or your money or your time.

When I was studying physics and chemistry in high school, I belonged to a group called Mathematics, Engineering & Science Achievement (MESA), and they had Rockwell engineers visit for an hour each week to tutor us. That really helped me. And when I sat on the Central Labor Council, successful adults were encouraged to be part of a program at a local elementary school. This program was embraced by a car dealership that would send its employees to sit with the children so that each child could practice reading to them. Any business can do that, and there are tons of programs out there that people can get plugged into. Of course, it's not always easy, because people are busy and have to think about their own problems and what they need to get done. But as the Rockwell engineers and those car dealership employees found out, an hour a week isn't a lot to sacrifice in return for providing others with tremendous benefits.

## LORETTA

At the government level, Hispanic Serving Institutions is another program where we've significantly increased the money in the federal budget to help those colleges that do a good job of recruiting and retaining those students, so that they will graduate. Some people say, "Why do you do that just for Hispanics?" and my answer is, "Well, we also do it at traditionally black universities and Native American universities, and now we do it at Hispanic universities because this is our workforce of tomorrow. Don't you want them educated? If you do, then we're going to have to figure out how we're going to keep them in school, and how we're going to make sure they stay in school and feel sufficiently comfortable in school to get good enough test scores to graduate, move on, and be the next set of leaders."

Our economic competitiveness has everything to do with how educated and how well trained people are, having the resources for research, and developing talent here as opposed to competing for talent. Accordingly, education is, in my opinion, a national security issue. However, because our education system is based at a local level, with local school boards controlling what happens in the classroom, I can't pass a piece of legislation at the federal level that says financial literacy must be taught in twelfth grade. I can pass a resolution that says the Congress believes it is important for it to be taught in twelfth grade, and we would love all schools to do so across the United States, but the decision for that to happen takes place in California, for example, at the state level, and then the local board has control of how it is implemented.

The point is, it's no longer about one high school graduate competing with another from across the city. Now it's about a high school graduate in Anaheim competing against a guy in India. So, this is a national security issue, because if we aren't economically competitive, we don't have to go to war to be weak. That's why I think we should be involved in education at the national level. Unfortunately, there's a philosophy, in particular from the Republican right, that there should be no involvement whatsoever at the federal level, and there aren't enough votes in Congress right now to overturn what's going on and enforce a certain investment in education for *all* children across America.

## LINDA

Making college more affordable is a huge issue. A lot of students who come from poor families may have the grades to get in, but they're afraid of the cost and they're really hesitant about taking a $12,000 loan each year to finance it. I counsel kids, "That's an investment in your education. That's an investment in *you*. Things come and go—you can lose your car in an accident or buy jewelry that ends up getting lost or stolen—but your education is something that can never be taken from you. And while it involves more sacrifice in the short term, it's an investment that pays greater rewards down the line."

Still, the fact that these young people have to start their adult life by accruing a huge debt is where, I think, our government has failed. I mean, the generation before me really benefited from the GI Bill and other sweeping programs that were basically education-friendly loans at a time when college fees were much more affordable and interest rates were far lower. That's no longer the case. The amount of debt that a student has to take on today is astronomical while the grants being issued are a lot smaller than they used to be because they haven't kept pace with inflation.

In 2007, we passed the Make College Affordable Act, which is the largest assistance program for higher education since the GI Bill. It increases the grants and decreases the interest that has to be paid on student loans, and it not only targets low-income families, but also those middle-class families who fall through the gaps when other assistance programs only benefit the very poor.

If you can give people equal economic opportunities and the ability to know what opportunities are out there, you're not only doing those people good, you're doing your society a lot of good in the long run. I always try to think in those terms. We shouldn't be content with the status quo. There's too much poverty in this country, there's too much exploitation, and I think people can make a fair profit and still treat employees well. The two are not incompatible.

Government offers the tools and the opportunities for people to succeed, but if we just go with corporate interests we might as well return to how things were during the late nineteenth century, when the robber barons owned everything and a country's wealth was in the hands of very few families. Democracy gets strangled when that happens because there can no longer be competing ideas or fair and open debate. And since the thing that makes American democracy great is the middle class, our democracy will suffer if that middle class is eliminated.

I'm not always convinced that when we pass laws in Congress, the people whom we have foremost in our minds are the hardworking folks who struggle to get by every day. This process is heavily influenced by very powerful interests that have a lot of money and a lot of clout, and people need to pay attention or those interests will dominate us. The ultimate power lies in the hands of those who vote, and as an optimist as well as a realist I am hopeful that, at some point in the not-too-distant future, we will wake up and understand that an investment in the human capital of this country is very much a worthwhile investment.

## LORETTA

At the same time, to share the wealth on a global level, I think this generation needs to focus on three pressing social issues: education, protection and regeneration of natural resources such as water, and infrastructure and communication. Instead of spending $3 billion a week in Iraq, we might be able to spend some of that on cleaning water sources around the world to improve hygiene and reduce the number of infant mortalities. We also might be able to spend some of that money on getting the Internet into villages where there isn't enough — or any — communication with the outside world, and helping to build critical road infrastructures so that people can travel, mail can be delivered, and market goods can be more easily transported.

We have the ability to invest in new technology so that a lot of underdeveloped areas can go through many of the same phases as we have in developing our nation. We can also send our people around the world to help with education, and generally we have the resources to provide other people with the assets that they need to become more productive in terms of crops and irrigation. We have the technology and know-how to really make a difference.

The world is small, and what happens in one country affects us in another, whether it's depletion of resources, climate change, or social unrest that sees people becoming so upset that they feel they have nothing to lose by hurting others whom they fear or believe are holding them down (i.e., terrorism). We are all interrelated, and those who have much, such as the United States, have the responsibilty to share the wealth and information to help others. By doing that, we'll become better people, and we'll also ensure a better future for our children.

# Acknowledgments

~

Writing a book is no small project. Accordingly, there are many people we have to thank for helping us make sure we actually finished the lengthy and time-consuming process. To our parents, Ignacio and Maria: thanks for your tough love and the sacrifices you made that helped us achieve what we have so far. To our brothers and sisters – Ignacio, Martha, Mike, Henry, and Frank – we can never thank you enough for the many discussions, interactions, and experiences that helped shape us as people and gave us the foundation to tell our stories.

Personally, I, Linda, would like to thank Jim Sullivan and his boys, Brendan, Jack, and Seamus. To Jim: thanks for reading the manuscript and making helpful suggestions. Thanks also for being supportive and positive throughout the process. To the boys: thanks for asking me a million questions and keeping me excited about this project!

To my incredible staff in Washington, D.C., and Cerritos, California: what can I say, except thanks for putting up with me, working so hard, and making me look good. Also, our grateful thanks to Ronn S. Davids for all his brilliant legal help in bringing this project to fruition.

I, Loretta, wish to thank all my current and former Washington, D.C., staff and my Orange County, California, staff, as well as my campaign staff, for all of their energy and for spreading great seeds of optimism and "can-do" attitude.

To my "White Boy Posse," those Anglo men who have believed in me and mentored me along very difficult roads. They include Stephen Simmons Brixey III, Gary Smith, Jim DeNoble, Dr. Daniel Heer, Dr. Harris Done, Dr. Neil Hollander, Jim Kenan, Larry Rolapp, Jim Doti, Greg Winterbottom, James Duff, Greg Willenborg, Wylie Aitken, Paul (41) Sentry, and Alan Mishne.

To my many girlfriends who provide a refuge when I need it and who push me when I hesitate – in particular, Donna Ashley, Sherial Heller, and Toni Blackstone, three very strong and caring women.

Thank you all for teaching me what being a friend is all about.

To Richard Buskin, we owe a great debt for keenly listening to us talk, distilling our words, and getting them down on the page because we were too busy. You kicked us in the pants to get this finished on time, no small feat when working with two women with such hectic schedules!

To Selina, our editor, who made us keep going even when the task looked daunting.

Finally, a big thanks to Linda Konner, our agent, who dreamed up this whole incredible project, and made sure that six years later, we *finally* got a chance to tell our story.

RICHARD BUSKIN is the *New York Times* bestselling author of fifteen books, on subjects ranging from Marilyn Monroe and Princess Diana to the Beatles, Phyllis Diller, and Sheryl Crow. Additionally, he is a journalist whose articles have appeared in newspapers and magazines around the world, including *Playboy*, the *New York Post*, the *Sydney Morning Herald*, the *Observer*, and the *Independent*. A native of London, England, he lives in Chicago with his daughter Melanie.